To: LesLee

Thank you for caring
enough to reach out and
help children of abuse.

Rosemary "Mercie" Adkins
November 15, 2013

Reflections of Mamie

A STORY OF SURVIVAL

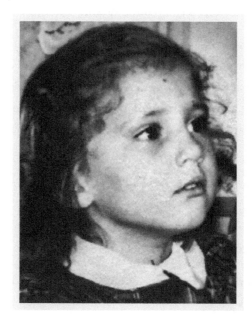

*Sad, afraid and alone, Mamie will show you how she
found her way so you can too.*

AVIVA
PUBLISHING

New York

ROSEMARY "MAMIE" ADKINS

Published by:
Aviva Publishing
Lake Placid, NY
518-523-1320
www.avivapubs.com

Address all inquiries to:
Rosemary Adkins
Reflections of Mamie
P. O. Box 4178
Bremerton, Washington 98312

Print ISBN: 978-1-938686-53-5

Library of Congress Control Number: 2013906429

Editor: Linda Hales
Cover image from childhood
Cover & Interior Design: Fusion Creative Works

For additional copies visit: www.Reflections-Of-Mamie.com

Printed in the USA

Readers Praise

"It has been my overwhelming pleasure to read and experience Reflections of Mamie. What a tragic childhood the author experienced. I felt, the whole time I was reading the first portion, that I wanted to just be there to protect little Mamie. Just to hug her and tell her she is loved. The author paints incredibly detailed scenes that quickly transported me there by her side. This is a book that makes you open your heart and see how wonderful life can eventually be, and how we can rise above anything. After reading I cannot help but apply Mamie's wisdom to my own life and family history of abuse and about how we can all leave the garbage-of-our-pasts behind, and move forward. I have and will continue to share my experiences after reading this book and my strong recommendation to anyone to enjoy this journey with Mamie."

Mike Foxworthy, Federal Way, WA

"*Reflections of Mamie: A Story of Survival* is an excellent five star memoir that is written in a highly engaging narrative form and I feel so fortunate that I had a chance to read it. It is a brave account of Mamie's experience of living through horrendous physical and emotional abuse as a child and young adult in the 50s and 60s. It is a story written to open the door of communication and provide an invitation, even a calling, to other victims of abuse to also share their story. Mamie writes about the difficulties she experiences in dredging up these frightening memories of abuse, but she also shares the need and relief she feels sharing her story rather than leaving the impact of the abuse buried deep within the interior of her psyche to haunt her and cause her further harmful stress.

One gets the idea from reading her story that if she can move out of abuse toward creating a positive environment with loving relationships in her adult life, that others can do the same. I love the way she addresses the reader throughout her sharing and brings you into her close confidence. It is this warm closeness with her readers in which she instills confidence and empowerment in anyone who has experienced abuse to be strong and work toward a better life through sharing with others whom they can trust.

I highly recommend this memoir for anyone who has experienced abuse as well as to anyone who needs to understand what people abused as children go through. This book says what many others will not say, reveals the abuse experience as it is lived, and leaves you with the clear understanding what you need in order to be sensitive and knowledgeable on this issue with anyone you might know who has been abused. I plan to recommend it in my coaching as an empowering example of a person who has found her strength in life despite the many hardships she endured and who understands the power of sharing one's life feelings with others who care and how that can lead to a transformation toward happiness.

Martha Love, Author of *What's Behind Your Belly Button?*
A Psychological Perspective of the Intelligence
of Human Nature and Gut Instinct

"*Reflections of Mamie* is a sad and joyous firsthand account of growing up under adversity. It is a story of survival during times of darkness that will leave you feeling Mamie's anguish. A must read for anyone with a difficult childhood or anyone wanting to understand the cycles of abuse!"

S. Allan Kane, Jr., M.D., California

"As a book reviewer, I've had the pleasure of reading many memoirs. Few have touched me with the purity of heart and soul presented by author Rosemary Adkins on the reflections of her life.

Author, "Mamie" narrates her memoir in such a way that it causes one to feel as if sharing a cup of tea and cookies with her, spellbound by the brutal honesty and innocence of a beautiful little girl. This sweet four-year-old child relates her lack of motherly love, and harsh physical and emotional abuse in heartbreaking renditions of her family life. Her quiet, pleasant father does not or will not stand up to his maniacal wife. One wonders if he's truly aware of what goes on during his long hours at work, or if he chooses to look the other way. Her older brother, Herb, is abused as well and does his best to protect his little sister, while the youngest son, J. Watson, is oddly doted upon by their strange and unpredictable mother.

Mamie talks directly to those reading her book, enveloping and including them into the sordid world of her youth. She has an endearing, chatty way of making one part of her world, clinging to her every word.

This precocious child as she grows up, gains an inner solid strength that makes her life bearable, even capable of holding on to hope . . . hope leading her to one day finding the love she was denied as a child. The road is long, full of trials, bumps and disappointments. The wounds are deep, causing ailments both physical and emotional. Mamie only grows stronger — becoming the antithesis of the one who refused to give her love — her own mother. In doing so she becomes the type of mother she herself so needed. This story is not a downer, due to the author's innate sense of humor and the light that she continually reaches for at the end of the tunnel.

This is one story that any reader interested in the survival of the abuses to the heart and spirit, will not want to miss. Will Mamie be able to hang onto her indomitable strength and spirit, or like so many others suffering abuse, will she slide back into a life of victimization?

The book has the added attraction of pictures of Mamie and members of her family which offers an even more visual closeness to her readers. If rated by deserved stars, they would shower from the sky like diamonds.

Micki Peluso, writer, journalist and author of
. . . And the Whippoorwill Sang

It is said "where there is no vision the people perish." Rosemary "Mamie" Adkins has rightly said she is a 'dreamer' and her dreams and visions reveal how much hope can come from what may seem to be the most hopeless of situations. In her book *Reflections of Mamie* she details the horror of being raised in a home without love as she speaks of the abuse that she experienced. Sadly, there is no doubt that her story has been seen in other families, and I would recommend this book to those who are seeking to know the answers from those trials of life.

Rosemary speaks quite frankly about how she felt within herself as a young child seeking to cope with both the emotional and physical scars of life that no one should have to endure at such a young age. She also details the way she discovered help from her 'special friends' who were there when she needed them. Today, as an adult, Rosemary "Mamie" Adkins blossoms as she pursues her goals in life by keeping her dreams and visions alive.

Jon Magee, author of *From Barren Rocks to Living Stones* **& *Paradise Island, Heavenly Journey***

Dedication

To my wonderful husband, **Douglas Earl Adkins**, who has been my 'rock' and my 'partner in life' through twenty-five years of wedded bliss. He has far exceeded his vow to keep me in sickness and in health and to be a loving Father to our beautiful daughter, Kecia. Without his love and support, this book would never have been written. For that matter, it was with Doug's love and encouragement that I was able to write my first book, 'Extraordinary Dreams of an Ireland Traveler'. Yes, my handsome blue-eyed sweetheart helped me to overcome a lifetime of abuse and encouraged me to share my story to free my soul and finally live in peace. "Thank you darling and know that I will love you always."

Kecia Kim Adkins Doke, our sweet and amazing daughter came into this world in need of a loving family who would cherish her forever. From the time that our precious little bundle was placed in my arms until this very day, she has enriched our lives in more ways than I can possibly count. My darling daughter has accomplished major milestones in her young life and made us the proudest parents in the universe. Kecia has stood by my side through so many of life's challenges and I could always count on her very able support in establishing my many charitable endeavors. "Thank you Kecia for encouraging me to finish this book."

Herbert Charles Hazen, my hero who I love with my whole being. He protected me at his own peril because he too was abused by that person who dared to call herself a 'Mother'. Hero, best friend, protector…yes, he was all those things and so much more to me. Indeed, it was Herb's 'all embracing' love that carried me through the darkest of times and gave me the strength to hold on when other children might have given up. In his refuge, I was able to find peace and in his innocence, the courage to fight and never give up. My sweet Herb was only five years older than I, yet the only true adult that I looked up to. Today we are both happy and at peace. "Thank you my dear Herb for loving me."

J. Watson, is my younger brother by eleven and a half months. Even as a young boy, he did what he could to support our family in the best way he knew how and always put his best foot forward. Our life's journey has been long and difficult but we managed to make it through with our sibling love intact. "If you only knew how happy I am that you never had to suffer the same abuse that Herb and I endured nor ever had to witness the worst of it. I love you my sweet brother and always have. You are a special man with many great qualities and I am proud to have you as my brother."

Ganelle Flower Swanson Ruzika, was my dearest friend and confidante of forty-three years. Ganelle succumbed to her lengthy battle with cancer in 2010 and will forever remain a driving force in my life. I'll never forget her persistent encouragement to write this book for the benefit of others. I'll miss you forever my friend...our late night talks, our laughter and our memorable walks on the beach. Thank you for being my guardian angel.

Sandy Adkins, our precious chocolate lab passed away on March 22, 2013. We loved her from the first moment we met until she left us too soon just days ago. Our baby girl brought more joy into our lives than we ever could have hoped for and we'll miss her forever.

Special Thanks

*To my many friends who hold a special place in my heart
and share a bond that can never be broken.
Thank you for giving me your support, guidance and hope.*

Linda Hales - I extend special thanks to my dear friend, author of *Sunshine and Her Big Blarney Smile!*, Sunshine: I'll Make You Smile! and *Andy-Roo: The Birthday Surprise!* Linda writes beautifully illustrated children's stories for the very young child, each with an age appropriate moral to enrich their learning experience. Linda's Andy-Roo is the proud recipient of the 2013 Kart Kids Book List Award for recommended reading. All of her books are sold on Amazon.com. More information and links can be found on her website, at: www.linnieslittlebooks.com Linda's strong dedication and support kept me on track throughout the painful process of bringing my book to its conclusion. Thank you Linda for your editing skill, musical research and timeline auditing. Most of all, your friendship, patience, compassion and loyalty will be cherished throughout eternity.

Yivian Liao is a gifted student artist/illustrator. Yivian illustrated Linda's newest Sunshine book, launched in March 2013 and my bookplate for Reflections of Mamie. I would certainly recommend her work to anyone looking for talent and a natural gift for inter-preting design needs from concept to conclusion. Both Linda and I have been issuing new challenges to Yivian and in each and every case, she has superceded our expectations. "Thank you Yivian for your magical flare for design." Email: yivian168@hotmail.com

Shiloh Schroeder & Jessi Carpenter are highly talented graphic designers who worked through both of my writing projects with the utmost flexibility and timeliness. Their work includes, but is not limited to the production of promotional materials, website and book cover design and interior formatting. Fusion Creative Works came highly recommended to me and I'm happy to do the same. "Thank you for your innate abilities, hard work and patience." www.FusionCW.com

Yvonne and Lester Adkins – *parents to my husband Douglas.* I can't begin to express how much I appreciate the warmth and love that Yvonne and Lester brought into my life that very first day we met. Doug took me home to meet his parents who accepted me into their hearts without reservation. I must say that I have been the luckiest bride in the world for 25 years, thanks to the Adkins, who taught me what it means to belong to a healthy, functional family, unlike the one that I grew up in. "This book would not be complete without acknowledging the love that you have brought into my life." I would also like to thank Doug's siblings and their spouses David, Aline and Wayne, Gail and Joe, Russell and Donna and Brian and Jan. "You are all worth your weight in gold!"

To **Allan *(Rusty)* Kane, MD.,** who has been my rock throughout the difficult writing of my book. Rusty was there for me, volun-teering his input, support and loyalty throughout every step of this difficult writing journey. He has been a true friend to me whenever I needed one. "Thanks Rusty! Your gentle nudging helped me to stick with it until my work was done."

To **Michael Foxworthy**, another wonderful friend who spent endless hours with me discussing techniques for writing my book. Mike is a wonderful writer who acquired his immense skill from his father, the renowned Author, Bruce Foxworthy. I am honored to be his friend and to have benefitted from his immense expertise. Mike was an amazing source of strength as I worked through the traumatic memories of my childhood so that this book could finally be written. "Your 'brotherly' friendship means the world to me Mike."

To **Diane Hazen, Catherine Lang, Bonnie McIntosh, Martha Wright, Robert and Cheryl Punt, George Evanoff, MD., Yuen San Yee, MD., Donald Bright, MD., Buck Hartford, PAC., Jon F. Hillyer, MD., Christopher Johnson, MD., Brian Wicks, MD., and Todd Schneiderman, MD. Authors: Sharla Shults, Martha Char Love, Micki Peluso, Mary Firmin, Clayton Bye, Peggy Strack, Ginny Cash and Kenneth Weene.** To each of you, I give my sincere thanks for believing in me with your encouragement, education and support. Many of you have read my unedited chapters without complaint and offered your help along the way. I am forever thankful for your gracious support in finishing my book after so many years on the drawing board. "I love you all dearly."

Acknowledgments

It has been my great fortune to have met Charles Suniga, a supremely talented composer, recording artist and producer of some of the world's most beautiful piano melodies. As a devoted 'Charles' fan, I am especially moved by the selections on his latest album, 'Moments of Peace'. Indeed, his peaceful music brought inspiration, calm and serenity as I wandered down this broken road of life to write my book. "Thank you Charles. Your music is in my heart and will remain there for eternity." www.MomentsOfPeace.com

Dreamcatchers

FOR ABUSED CHILDREN

DID YOU KNOW...

- 1 in every 3 girls will be sexually molested before the age of 18

- 1 in every 6 boys will be sexually molested before the age of 18

- Every 10 SECONDS a child is raped or killed in the U.S.

- Today up to 5 children will die from abuse or neglect

- In 13 seconds, another child will be abused in the U.S.

- There were 2.9 million child abuse reports made in 1992

- ONLY 28% of the children identified as harmed by abuse are investigated

- 85% of the 1.2 – 1.5 million runaways are fleeing abuse at home

- Today 6 children will commit suicide

- Suicide is the 3rd leading cause of death (ages 15-24)

- Untreated child abuse increases the likelihood of arrest for a violent crime by 38%

- 60 million survivors are former victims of child sexual abuse in America today

- 38% of women & 20% of men have been sexually abused during adolescence

- It is estimated that 3% - 6% of the clergy population has abused a child

- The typical child sex offender molests an average of 117 children…most of whom do not report the offense

Imagine the outcry if these statistics represented a disease, which was wiping out 5 children per day, victimizing millions, and whose by-products were disabilities and expanding violence. Youth rights are really about human rights, and simple empathy is a giant first step to the benefits of increased awareness. The high jump in child abuse statistics shows the importance of youth rights by showing cases of frightening lack of knowledge!

Because I am a strong supporter of child abuse victims, I have elected to share my donations between child and animal abuse charities.

FAIR USE ACT:

SOURCES:

www.childhelpusa.org
www.childwelfare.gov
www.child-abuse-effects.com
www.safehorizon.org
www.helpguide.org
www.ehow.com/how_10872_prevent-child-abuse.html

Please help stop abuse and love your children.

For further information please contact Dreamcatchers at: www.dreamcatchersforabusedchildren.com

Humane Society

Animals are among life's most precious gifts and are deserving of the same love and care that we give our children. I can't begin to count the ways that our pets have enriched our lives and those of the sick and elderly. Thanks to all volunteers who work tirelessly to save injured, lost, abandoned and abused animals. Because I am a strong supporter of animal rescue teams, I have elected to share my donations between child and animal abuse charities.

KITSAP HUMANE RESCUE SOCIETY

Mission:
Rescue, Rehabilitate, Rehome.

Kitsap Humane Society is an independent, non-profit charitable organization committed to providing life-changing solutions to people and companion animals. KHS does so by:

- Accepting, sheltering and rehabilitating companion animals in need.

- Providing humane rescue, protection, prevention, adoption and education services.

- Implementing progressive life-saving and life-affirming programs.

- Collaborating and partnering with our region and supporters to build a model humane community.

During 2012, Kitsap Humane Dociety (KHS) overcame major organizational and public relations challenges and rebuilt the organization while continuing to provide outstanding care for the animals.

Kitsap Humane Society has maintained a
94% lives saved/6% euthanasia rate.

VOLUNTEER/FOSTER CARE

The Kitsap Humane Society relies heavily on volunteers who provide daily care, socialization and training for thousands of animals, increasing their adoptability.

- 2012 began decline in volunteer hours, but by spring, volunteer hours were on the upswing.

- Foster caregivers contributed 5,739 foster hours in December alone for at-risk and very young animals.

OPINION/COMMENT OF AUTHOR

If you have a love for animals, care to protect their lives and have extra time, please consider helping this agency or agencies in your area to save their lives. Donate as you can with time, food or money because together, we can stop the waste of precious life. Help rescue abused and abandoned animals by supporting your local animal shelters and thank those who work so hard serving your community to preserve the wellbeing of pets.

Fun Facts of 1947

MONDAY, SEPTEMBER 29ᵀᴴ, THE DATE THAT MAMIE WAS BORN

Famous Facts

- President Harry Truman (1884-1972) make the first-ever televised presidential address from the white House

- Altie Taylor, soccer star

- R. J. Evans, FBA, Historian

- Martin Ferrero, American Actor

- Jon Snow, British TV Journalist (Channel 4)

- Lyndon Harrison, MEP

- The Hughes Flying Boat, the Spruce Goose, piloted by designer Howard Hughes on its first and only flight

- Gas – 15 cents per gallon

- Bread – 13 cents per loaf

- Average House Price - $6,600.

- Average Wage - $2,850. Per year

- U.S. Postage stamp – 3 cents

TRIVIA

- Dizzy Gillespie presented his 1st Carnegie Hall concert in New York

- Former Yankee manager Joe McCarthy signs to manage Red Sox

- Record World Series crowd of 73,365 at Yankee Stadium ($325,828)

- In 1951 there were 15 million Americans that owned TV sets and my family was lucky enough to enjoy one by 1955. Before that time they enjoyed listening to radio shows like "Amos and Andy."

Contents

Introduction

First of all, if you are a victim of abuse, be it emotional, mental or physical, IT IS NOT YOUR FAULT! It matters little if you are a child, adult, male or female, abuse is not an acceptable way of life and it is never your fault. If you are an adult and find yourself in this situation, get out! If you are a child, it is more difficult but you can get help…talk to a friend, teacher, church clergyman, police or anyone who holds a position of trust. A spanking for bad behavior does not constitute abuse but a beating is quite another matter.

Abuse, as defined in most dictionaries, is improper or excessive use of treatment or defamation of character through mental abuse, none of which is acceptable.

Abuse is an ugly thing no matter what form it takes. In Webster's Dictionary, abuse is explained as follows: 'a corrupt practice or custom obsolete; a deceitful act: deception; language that condemns or vilifies usually unjustly, intemperately, and angrily; physical maltreatment'.

PLEASE make no mistake, if you have been abused as a child in any way, especially over long periods of time, you must first become free in your spirit BEFORE having children of your own. YOU must first rid yourself of the demons inside you so that you don't risk passing the damage onto your own children and precipitate generational abuse. YOU and only you can make that wise decision.

It took me thirty eight (38) years to be sort of free but fifty four (54) years before I was finally beyond it. It didn't happen until my heart and spirit were ready to accept real love and believing that I deserved it, that I corrected my outlook and began to make wise choices. Only then was I able to recognize a good thing when I saw it. It was then that I met my husband who gave my daughter and I, his devotion, patience, love and commitment forever. It took some time but the day did come when my thoughts were finally free of anxiety, fear and doubt and it came as a revelation that I was indeed, a decent human and worthy of love.

Thank God for love, trust and forgiveness. I only wish I could undo all of the mistakes I made when my heart was so sad instead of lusting for love to fill the void caused by emptiness and rejection. I had many chances to find my way but never saw them as I was too consumed with the grief of never being loved by my mother. I watched her give all her love to my younger brother while my older brother and I meant nothing to her. I suffered her words over and over again. "Why can't you be like your younger brother? Why do you have to be such a huge disappointment? Why can't you just vanish like you do when your father leaves? You'll never mean anything to me!"

I hated her yet loved her for what she was supposed to be to me. Her constant belittlement soon became the image that I held of myself and that can take a lifetime to turn around.

INTRODUCTION

Keep a journal, help someone else, love a pet, find yourself because YOU ARE WORTH IT and deserve to be happy. Love will come to you—just LET IT IN!

Before we get started, the story I'm about to tell is a true reflection of my life. It is as difficult to tell as it was to live through. It took sixteen agonizing years to recover the horrific memories that I thought were hidden from the light forever. I tried but failed to tell my story in the third person but it only served to prevent me from facing the inevitable trauma head on. Instead, I chose to exorcise my demons by writing in the first person, up close and personal as I relived the horrors of my childhood. Some of what you are about to read will be upsetting but it is the only way that I can reach out to those in need.

As we progress through Mamie's life, I show you how desperate I was to escape from my Mother's hateful abuse and how my failed attempts led me down the path of destruction more often than not. And all of this was because of the deprivation of my mother's love.

I pray you will find your special place to be as Mamie did for many years—your personal space where you can drown out your pain and sorrow. For me, that was sandy beaches and the call of the sea. That is where I found my sustenance until I was able to become the wholesome person that I had always yearned to be.

My parents were Jack and Sara and I grew up with two brothers… Herb, who was five years my senior and J. Watson, only eleven and a half months younger. Together, we walked a path in life that most will never encounter.

You'll want to stay with me to the end as 'Mamie' fights her battles, dreams her dreams and plans her escapes from the disaster that was her life. Perhaps you will see yourself somewhere between these pages but in any case, you'll get to decide if and how she was able to pick up the pieces and make a success of her life.

In the old country where my mother's heritage began, it is a cultural belief that a woman who gives birth to boys is considered to be of value and those who bore a girl were to be shunned. According to Mother, she held to that belief or so she claimed. Although she was born and raised in America, she claimed to share those cultural values. Now, isn't that interesting? Considering that she had three sisters and no brothers, she had nothing to compare her life to. A better question might be, how did she reconcile her contempt for her first born son? Those questions will never be answered as the relevant members of her family are no longer among the living!

My father Jack, was quite the opposite personality type than my Mother, Sara. He was a quiet man who rarely shared his opinions but more importantly, would never speak up to or against his wife no matter what he believed was right.

He was a hardworking man whose careers were almost too many to list but to better understand him, here are just a few occupations that Jack worked at in his lifetime: he was known as a real estate wizard, a donut and fudge maker, oil field worker, swap market worker, gold and diamond designer, restaurant supply owner and his favorite was a second hand store owner! His only real shortcoming was his lack of back bone, especially his inability to protect his children from his abusive wife. She was simply cruel and hateful and we all suffered in one way or the other.

Many other people played significant roles in my life and in this book. One of the first you will meet is Colena, who hailed from the small town of Cold Springs, Texas. She was our nanny, housekeeper, amazing cook and stand-in mother! To this day, I need only close my eyes to be reminded of her protective words, "Miss Sara, Miss Sara, please don't hit my baby no more."

Among the people who made the greatest impact in my life are my husband of almost twenty-five years, our precious daughter, Kecia and Herb, my older brother who also suffered insane abuse at our mother's hand. Other special mentions were Daniel of Del Ray Beach, Florida, Ganelle of Oregon, and my dear friends in Bremerton, Washington.

Happily, after many years of bitterness, jealously, rage and disappointment, I'm proud to add my younger brother, J. Watson, to the list of people who influenced my life in a positive way. J. Watson was the one sibling who had it all while Herb and I had nothing. It was not his fault because he was only a child, but later in life, he came forward and apologized for allowing me, his only sister to be beaten for things that were not of my own doing. In his own way, he too was a victim. Many years later, his family confided in me how it had tortured his heart to remember the cruelty that Herb and I suffered through. Counseling was the only way that helped him to find peace with it.

Charles and Jeanine of *'Moments in Peace'* renown, helped to put me on my path to peace through their inspired music. As a result, I was able to write more objectively without the extreme emotions that had previously interrupted the process. I also give much credit to the music of the sixties for freeing up so many memories that had long been forgotten.

My reflections will reveal the many ways that my mother destroyed my self-esteem. How demeaning it was to be told such things as, "You're a miserable nothing and you'll never amount to anything but dirt that gets swept into the trash." This and an untold number of insults were hurled at me until the day that she died but I have since recovered from the damage and they no longer haunt my soul. I'm still amazed at how my life has turned around and question what I ever did to deserve such happiness. I only need to think of my precious family to remind me that I have endured and prevailed over the damage that she did to me as a child. When I need to be reminded that I really am lovable, I go to my answering machine to listen to the many saved messages from my daughter, each one ending with, 'I love you Mom'.

The story you are about to read is a true account of my history of abuse. Please know that I struggled tremendously as I tried to sort out event timelines, especially from my early childhood. I am satisfied that I have succeeded in doing so. In many instances, I changed names to protect the true identities of persons who played roles in my story.

If you have suffered any type of abuse, PLEASE, NEVER GIVE UP! I am living proof that you can survive the tragedies in your life if only you take that advice. Death is final and if you do take that road, you will never know the peace and love that can be yours if only you determine to find it. If you stumble, then just keep trying and it will all be worth it in the end because you matter. Be happy and let love in and the sorrow out.

Come along now and follow my footsteps. You will learn how I found my way out and managed to mend my broken spirit.

Always remember -NEVER GIVE UP.

Blessings to all my friends!

Mamie

1

In the Beginning

WHY CAN'T MY MOMMY LOVE ME?

Now I lay me down to sleep
I pray the Lord my soul to keep
If I should die before I wake
I pray to God my soul to take

IN THE BEGINNING

ALONE, AFRAID, UNWANTED AND ABUSED…

These are the sentiments of a four year old child whose name was 'Mamie' and who silently prayed to God that he would let her come home and live with HIM. Alone, afraid, unwanted and abused, she learned to stand alone.

WHERE I CAME FROM…

Let me begin by introducing you to my family so that you may have a glimpse of who they are and how they fit into my story. You will learn about my parents and two brothers and a bit about my grandparents and the Lebanon connection.

My mother, Sara, was a strikingly beautiful woman with lovely brown hair and eyes and medium build. She was admired by many for her great sense of style and sophistication. But that is not the Sara I knew. I sometimes thought of her as a Jekyll and Hyde monster who could move in an out of character in a flash! Sara had her public persona which was reserved for the outside world and a dark side, witnessed only by her family…cold, conniving and sadistic. Quite simply, that is who she was and who she would be until her dying day!

My father, Jack, was quite the opposite. He was a quiet, hard-working family man about five foot eleven with brown hair. He kept his opinions to himself and rarely stood up to his wife, Sara, who always managed to prevail, no matter what. You might say that my father was the proverbial 'Jack' of all trades, a versatile, multi-talented man who had worked in many fields, whatever it took to support his wife and operating a second-hand store. So it came as no surprise, that he was dubbed with many nicknames…*Diamond Jack, Junk Man Jack and fudge maker to name a few.*

Herbert Charles was my older brother by five years. He was a handsome boy with soft brown hair and eyes. How I loved Herb's eyes because his sweetness and sincerity shone through so brightly, revealing the goodness in his heart, though if you looked deeply enough, you might also tap into the pain and suffering that he had grown up with at Sara's hands. Herb was my hero and my protector, the only one who dared to love me unconditionally, for which he paid a very high price. Oh, indeed he did! I'll tell you later why mother sent him away.

J. Watson, my younger brother by a year, was quite another story! He was a small, sweet boy, with medium brown hair and eyes, yet timid and quiet like his father. J. Watson was our mother's favorite child, who was on the receiving end of her excessive doting which she reserved especially for him, her last born child. At his young age, he had no way of knowing why he was the only one of us who our mother ever loved but thankfully, that understanding would come many years later. Outside the house was a different story. Being tiny and not very street smart, he was targeted by bullies on the way home from school. Big sister to the rescue though…yes, that would be me! I fought off his tormenters who eventually learned that it didn't pay to pick on J. Watson.

My mother's parents preferred to be known as Aunt Rosie and Daddy Sam, not wishing to be remembered as 'grand' anything at all. They were from the old country, Lebanon specifically. Aunt Rosie hailed from Beirut and she loved to remind anyone who would listen, that her grandfather was a Bishop, no less. Daddy Sam, came from a wealthy family, who happily paid a handsome dowry for Rosie's hand in marriage. They would have four children, my mother Sara and her three sisters, whose names will remain anonymous out of respect for the one remaining daughter from that union. I swear that this remaining sister inherited the same gene as Sara; after all, she was just as cold and mean. My fondest memory was when Aunt Rosie taught me how to belly dance around the kitchen table as she cooked her beloved Lebanese cuisine. As I recall, she also taught me how to dance the Dabki, another well-known Lebanese folk dance. How could I ever forget that?

My father's parents were far less colorful but they do have a rightful home in this section of my book. Dad's mother, Mary, died when I was a toddler, about 3 years old. His father, John Watson, died much earlier from surgical complications when Dad was a young boy. Being the eldest of their four children, including a brother and two sisters, it fell upon my father's shoulders to quit school and support his family. They may have been poor, but from what I understand, they were happy.

I was named Rosemary after my maternal grandmother, 'Rose' and my paternal grandmother, Mary. My nickname 'Mamie' was coined by my baby brother, J. Watson, who was unable to pronounce my name. So, now that you know my family better, I'll move forward to tell 'Mamie's story!

HELLO…MY NAME IS MAMIE AND
THIS IS MY STORY…

Though painful, my memory permits me to travel back to where I once lived. We were a family of five and living in Bellair, a small suburb of Houston, a modest community that originated in 1918. We lived at 5002 Chestnut Street in a pleasant neighborhood yet little did most of our neighbors know what went on behind the closed doors of our seemingly happy little home. I remember that little house so well. It was built in 1954 for my family. The exterior was painted a soft grey and white…even the inside walls were white throughout. It had three bedrooms, one bath and was equipped with an attic fan to battle the unbearable heat of the summer months. Even the walls were damp from the relentless humidity. As I tell you this, I can still feel the sweat across my brow and shudder at the memory of roaches reigning their terror across our floors. Oh my gosh, those things frightened me so!

And that is not a reflection of my mother's housekeeping skills—quite the opposite. In fact, my mother would never tolerate even a hint of dirt in her house or on any of her children. Cleanliness was an obsession with her which I suspect was just another one of those southern things.

THE BEGINNING...

My earliest memories of mother's domination still torture me to this day. How can I ever forget my nanny's urgent pleas as they echoed throughout our house, "Miss Sara, Miss Sara, please don't hit my baby no more!"

Now I'm shivering— it's so cold and I am so afraid. I don't want to play alone in the cold. I want my mommy to come out and play with me? I love my mommy. Oh mommy, why have you left me out here all alone? Other children ask me, "Where is your mommy? I cry when I watch across the street and see their mommy's and daddy's having a delightful time playing with them, frolicking and making angels in the snow. I built this snowman and my legs are cold and my hands hurt so badly. I used up all of the snow to build this snowman to make her proud of me. I want her to see it but I can't find her. Is she lost? She must be here somewhere. I need her to hold me and love me because I am cold and she needs to warm me. Has she abandoned me? Won't someone help me? Should I hide somewhere until my mommy comes back for me? I don't want anyone to take me away? Maybe she's inside where it is warm with my baby brother!

Okay, now my special friends are here and they will protect me. They make me happy when I am afraid and will never let anything or anyone hurt me. I wondered if they would always watch over me.

Such are the thoughts that have ravaged my soul for many decades, forever wondering just where my mommy was when I needed her so desperately. So, confused and bewildered, I found refuge in my older brother's arms and those of my special friends who came when I beckoned.

Herb, my older brother loved me unconditionally and protected me like a parent but he was only a child himself. He too suffered because of the emotional absence of our mother.

Sitting on the concrete porch out front and feeling so cherished by my brother and my special friends, seemed like salvation itself. It was such fun giggling when my brother would tickle me! He would so often say to me, "Mamie, I'll always love and protect you."

These were precious memories yet so many still remain hidden in the darkest corners of my mind. I felt that I was the luckiest sister in the world for having a brother who loved me enough to stay by my side rather than go off and play with friends his own age. He had a special way of making my sadness more bearable and it still warms my heart whenever I reflect back in search of anything worth smiling about. Yes indeed, Herb was my hero and the only living soul who I was able to count on in my childhood.

I wanted so badly to run into my Daddy's arms when Mommy was hurting me but I could never find him when that was happening. Where did he go? Couldn't he hear my cries? "Daddy, why didn't you keep me safe?"

Happiness was a confusing concept at best, never completely understood by Herb and I. We only knew what we wanted and needed more than anything else in the world. We had witnessed it daily by the example our mommy had set with our baby brother, always pampering him and showering him with copious amounts of love and affection.

As I write this, I am struggling with all of my heart to revisit the broken path that Herb and I walked and pray that none of you have ever been in that place.

2

Early Memories

Try as I might, I can't seem to recall much from my first three years of life, other than bare snippets of events which made a dramatic impact on my development. "My mother told me very little about my earliest years but I'll share these memories with you so that you may get to know me from the beginning."

I was often reminded of when I was a toddler, barely two years old, I would steal my baby brother's bottle before he had a chance to finish it. The tone of those reminders was such that I had committed the unforgivable sin, even at that tender age. Now I find myself wondering if this behavior was simply my way of revisiting the warmth and security that a warm bottle represents to a child who was still a mere baby herself or indeed, if it was only a fabrication to hurt my feelings.

According to my mother, my father nearly ran me over with his car when I was only three. It seems that I was playing in the driveway behind his vehicle and he didn't see me until it was nearly too late. This near tragedy shook him up so badly, he took the day off work to build a fence to keep me from wandering off into harm's way. Looking back, my father's concern for my safety was borne out of love, though he rarely expressed it as such.

Those were a few of my earliest recollections, yet I sense that I may have blocked out far more than I'll ever remember. From time to time, an event will trigger a memory in vivid detail. It might be an event that I witnessed, perhaps read about or even a song on the radio and I would be taken back to that space and time when it occurred. Even to this day, when it happens, a dark cloud infuses my entire being for days on end, until I am finally able to rise above it and put it to rest.

Much of what happened after that was both unforgivable and un-forgettable. No child, at any age, should have to bear the abuse that mother inflicted upon Herb and I. When I was around four, I rationalized what I can only interpret as being a sad revelation—Mommies must only love their children when they are babies and love ceases to exist once the next little baby comes along. That was how I made sense of it from my childish perspective, given that my mother devoted all of her love and attention to my baby brother.

By the time I was about four, I no longer felt a connection or any sense of emotional nourishment as a member of my family. Gosh, how I prayed as a little girl, for God to make my mommy love or even just like me. My only importance in her world was to have me watch over my baby brother, yet if anything ever went wrong, she blamed it on me. As punishment, I was often sent outside to play alone, even on the coldest days. Thank goodness, my father saw to it that I donned a coat and mittens before being shoved out the door. And then would begin one of those long, cold and lonely episodes that were commonplace in my young life.

My mother's abuse knew no mercy or age boundary. She was hard and mean spirited toward Herb and I, never letting an opportunity go by without reminding us of how worthless we were and that she would be better off if we had never been born. Her verbal abuse often escalated to a physical level, depending upon her mood. There were even times when she appeared to derive great pleasure from slapping me in the face and beating me with a leather belt on my upper legs to hide the crimson welts that would remain inflamed for many hours and even days. Though faded over time, I still carry some of those scars even today. Such was my life but I could never understand why it had to be that way.

J. Watson was never punished but then, why should any of us have been—after all, we were only babies. She was the adult but always found reasons to justify her outbursts of temper. I often wondered why I didn't hate her, though there were times that I thought I did or realized that I should have. Even when I uttered those words, I knew that deep in my heart, I loved her unconditionally—she was my mommy for goodness sake!

In those days in the South, prejudice against the colored population was still rampant. Derogatory terms such as 'coloreds, Negroes, and niggers' were the lingo of the day and all too often, used in the most cruel and hurtful manner. Just before we moved to Angelton, when I was only five, my nanny Colena took me to a café for lunch. When we entered, she was told she could not sit at the table with me. "Coloreds aren't allowed in here missy," the waiter said to me, as though I would understand what he meant by that. Even at my young age, I had a strong sense of purpose and right from wrong. I wasn't about to stand for this kind of treatment, and being the rebellious child that I was, I let him know it in no uncertain terms. I blurted out, "You may not be a 'nigger' lover but I love her! She's my mommy and that means she eats with me and not at some back table." And I didn't stop there. "If she has to eat there then we're leaving and I'll tell everyone in town that you threw a little white girl out of your restaurant!" I was so loud, that he quickly sat us down and begged me to stop talking.

I had no way of knowing that it was wrong to use the 'n' word and I surely meant nothing by it. I loved Colena so much and I would never have intentionally hurt her in any way. Later, she lovingly explained to me that these were not nice names and that I should not talk that way ever again. I listened and obeyed—I never did it again. She was my mommy now and I knew that she loved me.

Shortly after that incident, my family moved to the small town of Angelton, about forty-three miles from Houston. Shortly after we moved there, my father was injured in a serious accident, which kept him from working for a long time. Now, it was my mother's turn to earn a living to bring much needed money into our household. Realizing that she had no work skills, she decided to bake cakes and pies and sell them. She was very good in the kitchen and especially enjoyed baking. It didn't hurt that she had Colena's help. Our nanny Colena, lived with us on week days and she could cook like an angel.

I loved Colena and remember that she cooked the best food ever made and the whole family would attest to that. Even at the ages of four, five and ten, we each got to enjoy our favorite desserts. Colena knew that during the bad times, it was the only sure way to raise our spirits. I understood that Colena loved me like she was my real mother and that she would always be my friend. She used to say that someday she would return as an angel and watch over me.

Colena had taught my mother to bake and she was good at it so this was how she was to earn the money we needed to get by while Daddy was recovering.

Her delectable desserts were sold to friends and bakeries in town and were in heavy demand by the local townsfolk. In the minds of three young children though, it didn't seem fair that we never got to enjoy any of it. Goodness, they smelled so good and I so wanted to savor some too. Well, it would seem that I had an overabundance of determination and grit because what I dared to do next did not sit well with my mother.

One night, J. Watson and I snuck into the kitchen to serve ourselves a midnight snack—well, a snack that turned into a feast, I'd have to say. We ate the middle out of every cake and pie on the table, waiting to be delivered in the morning.

The next morning, my mother beat me severely and despite the fact that J. Watson and I were both completely plastered in chocolate, I was the only one punished for the escapade. It seemed to her that I was the older of the two, and therefore, must be the ringleader of the crime. This particular beating was so bad, that I pleaded with her, "Please stop mommy, please." But it was a very long wait before she did.

The next night, all I could think about was the temptation to do it all over again. It was nearly impossible to resist that sweet aroma wafting from the kitchen and so I dared to brave another raid, despite the almost certain knowledge, that my punishment would be even more harsh than the first time. Oh yes, you bet it was.

After the second time, mother installed a gate across the doorway to the kitchen and placed the sweet treasures well out of harm's way. Herb was away visiting our grandparents, so mother only had J.

Watson and I to watch over. I'm sure that she believed the problem was resolved but two beatings and her additional security measures were not enough to stop us little thieves in the night! We struck yet again and stuffed our little faces until we could eat no more. Mother was fit to be tied, figuring that I must have lifted my brother over the gate and followed after him in order to impede her efforts. This time, I was whipped so badly that I bore deep, angry welts on my back and both hips which lasted for weeks. She claimed that the reason J. Watson was not punished was because I forced him to participate in the eating sprees.

With that final beating, I managed to quell my appetite for my mother's desserts once and for all. Had I not been sent to bed hungry so often, my kitchen visits may never have happened. Nothing stopped me from craving Colena's treats though. I still remember her butterscotch pie— oh yum! To this day, I believe her sweet treats represented the warmth and love that I was so yearning to have from my mother.

Whenever Herb was home from our grandparents, he would take his share of abuse along with me. Being the biggest though, he was able to escape from time to time. He would try to protect me as best he could, but it was usually a losing battle. For reasons only known to my mother, she forever dubbed me the instigator and on such occasions, Herb and I both suffered at her hands.

My memories of her beatings will haunt me forever. Mommy's yelling and my screams could be heard throughout the entire house, but no one was ever home to help me, except Colena and sometimes Herb. Colena would beg her to stop and her urgent pleas could often be heard throughout the neighborhood. I can still hear her screaming, "Miss Sara, Miss Sara, please don't hit my baby no more!"

Rarely a day went by without suffering at her hands. I became petrified of my mother and of life itself, always listening for the other shoe to drop. Oh my goodness, how I longed for affection and some happiness. Even a happy thought would have been a rare treat.

At night I would say my prayers, 'Now I lay me down to sleep, I pray the Lord my soul to keep… God bless Momma, Daddy, Herb and J. Watson. God bless everyone in our family and in my heart.' My mother was always standing next to me when I said my nightly prayer so I had to be careful to include her name. It always seemed so unfair that I had to pray for her when she hated me so much. After all, I didn't want God to bless her. I wanted Him to make her stop!

When I was old enough to have friends over after school, my mother would inevitably find a way to show more affection to them than to me. She would make it a point to shout in my face, "Why can't you be more like your friends!" Her taunting was relentless. "Why do you have to be so ugly and stupid?" At times she seemed more like a mother to them, cruelly making it a point to leave me out in the cold and feeling humiliated and alone. I longed so much to be the apple of her eye, to really matter to her but I was never good enough to win her approval.

Only once did my father dare to stand up to my mother to protect me. It was a futile attempt at best. He learned all too quickly that he couldn't win this battle and simply stopped trying. Instead, he would caution me to, "Stay out of her way so you don't get into any more trouble." Gee, I had loved my father so much and it seemed like he had cared about me too until he utterly let me down! When he completely stopped trying, I learned to resent him too. It seemed like I had nowhere left to turn.

Someone once told me how my mother would occasionally tell me that she loved me when I was very small,   How I wish I could remember that so I would know how it felt to be important to someone, especially her.   From the time I was a toddler, she would remind me that it would have been better had I been a boy too and that J. Watson was her only true love child…the only child worth her time! She loved him more than life itself and doted on his every need. I longed for that same love and attention, that she would hold me when I was sick and read stories to me at bedtime—just for me alone and not to be shared with my younger brother. Instead, she would remind me that, "I'm reading this for J. Watson and because your dad is home, I have to let you listen in but don't get used to it!" These were the times that my heart would break into a million pieces; and, these were the times that I would cry out to her, "Oh mommy, why do you hate me so much. You used to love me. What did I ever do to make you hate me?" I would hear myself crying out those pleas daily for many years.

A child needs to feel a parent's love at all times but whatever love my father tried to give to me, my mother would try even harder to deny it to me. It seemed that she had made it her mission to deprive me of any semblance of how good and nourishing that might feel to me.

Then, there was the day that I had to stay home from kindergarten because I was sick. My father wanted me to stay home so that I wouldn't make the other school children ill. He promised to stay home with me so that my mother wouldn't treat me so badly, but, wouldn't you know, she managed to find a way around that too. She sent my dad out on errands and I found myself home alone with her. He had no sooner closed the door behind him when she made a beeline to my room. First, she dragged me by the hair out of my bed, cursing loudly, that I had ruined her day and that, "Someone has to earn a living in this house and if the bills don't get paid, it'll be your fault for making someone stay home with you."

My punishment for being sick that day hurt me more than I can ever say. My mother demanded that I do her housework since Colena was off with her own family. I truly tried my best to do a good job so that maybe she would let me go back to bed and get some rest. Instead, she followed me around, all the while admonishing me, "Hurry up before your dad gets home or I'll take a belt to your legs." I was only five years old and didn't know much about pushing a vacuum except when Colena would let me help her. But because my mother was a perfectionist where housework was concerned, I was horrified that she would find even a speck of dust that I might leave behind and her tirade would start all over again. Often, that meant striking me in the face repeatedly and later explaining to my father and anyone else who asked, that the bruises on my face were caused by my own clumsiness. As I recall, my face was bruised all too often yet she continued to get away with it. She always threatened that if I ever told anyone what really happened, I would be sorry, and believe me, she meant it!

It was those and other terrifying events that made me fear for my life when I was alone with my mother. When my family was home, it suited her just fine to pretend that I wasn't there or to fake that she cared anything at all. As pathetic as it may sound, even though I knew it was an act for the benefit of others, I still craved that love so desperately, that I inhaled it as though it were pure oxygen.

This was my fate and I lived it for many years. I would yearn for my mother's approval right up to the day that she died but I would never know how precious it could have been.

J. Watson never knew that when he and the rest of the family were out, our mother would take out her belt and whip me until I could no longer stand up. It took nothing at all for me to light her fuse, little if anything, to set her off against me. To this day, I carry faded scars on my hips and deep wounds in my heart that I fear will never heal. Whenever I relapse into my past, I can still hear Colena pleading, "Miss Sara, Miss Sara, please don't hit my baby no more!" Her words are and forever will be, emblazoned on my heart as though they were just spoken yesterday.

I so yearn to understand why my mother felt so much contempt for Herb and I, yet only love and affection for my younger brother, J. Watson. And even though she strictly forbade my father from loving and protecting us, there was no one to turn to except one another and our precious nanny, Colena. J. Watson was just too young to understand.

Each night, I went to bed in fear of the abuse that my mother would inflict on me the next day and the many tomorrows to come. Often, out of sheer panic, I'd run to either Herb or Colena's room to hide under their bed to escape my fear and to finally drop off to sleep with reasonable assurance that I would make it through the night unharmed.

Herb paid a heavy price for loving and shielding me, as only a young boy could. He was only 10 years old but he was my big brother and I loved him more than life itself. He represented everything sweet and good to me, everything that we had the right to expect from our parents. Sadly, most of his efforts were foiled, resulting in nasty beatings, comparable to what I had to endure on a daily basis. Often, he'd escape to grandma and grandpa's house, the only place that he was able to receive unconditional love and affection. But for him, that relief was short-lived when mother put an abrupt stop to his visits. She never knew when he might expose her for her unmerciful parenting and felt an urgent need to separate him from his grandparents. My mother's cruelty knew no bounds!

Barely a year younger than me, J. Watson was a shy, sweet and timid little boy. I learned much later that he was often on my side in those early years but kept it to himself. He got into the usual amount of mischief so typical of a little boy but never had to fear reprisal for any of his childish misdeeds. Mother always made it a point to tell him in front of Herb and I that he could never do anything to make her angry or disappointed. It mattered little that he should have been chastised for some of his misbehavior but instead, mother considered it to be cute and normal and rewarded him with copious amounts of affection. What I didn't understand was why she blamed his childish misdeeds on me. My punishment was usually a back hand to the face or a belt to the hips and legs while he would be excused as being just a growing boy. This regrettable family dynamic was persistent for many years. Is it any wonder why I developed a full blown resentment which lasted for many decades to come? Perhaps I was jealous of J. Watson because he never had to suffer at the hands of his mother in the way that Herb and I did but still, I'm so happy that he was never hurt.

"My dear reader, as I continue my search for memories to share with you, I try to focus on recalling some happy times." Oh yes, there were precious and few times that I can still smile about to this day, when I'd actually experience the joy that I always hoped would last.

The best times of all were spent at the ocean's edge where I could breathe in the clean salt air and allow my mind to wander, imagining that life could always be like this in my family. Unhappily, that dark shadow of dread followed me everywhere I'd go, forever threatening to steal away any joy before I had the chance to savor it.

Here's another special memory which I'm particularly fond of. While we were living in Angelton, mother befriended a woman whose name I believe, was Margaret. She helped mother to find a horse and provided room and board for it on her property. Now, we're talking about love at first sight here. I couldn't get enough of our new horse, who we named Baby Doll. Fortunately, Margaret had a particular fondness for me and I loved every minute that I spent at her house. Mother had no choice but to go along with that because she needed Margaret to advance her social and business status in the community. I often wonder whatever became of her.

These are but a few of my early memories that have haunted me throughout my life and that I hope can finally be put to rest.

3

On the Road Again

In Chicago
Back- Cousin Dan, Brother Herb
Front-Cousin Jane, Mamie, Brother J.Watson

I was at a stage in my life when I dreaded the summer months and the obligations that came along with it. As usual, work would demand that J. Watson and I sacrifice any prospect of cultivating a social life such as most children got to experience. Instead, summer was the time of year when mother and dad, J. Watson and I travelled the country, setting up department store displays for an artificial flower and wicker import business. Herb would spend his summer with our grandparents where he was able to enjoy some semblance of normalcy and make friends with other children.

Each product planogram was pre-programmed and it was our responsibility to set up the displays perfectly, according to the plan. I'm not surprised that we learned to become little perfectionists at such a young age, some of which has stuck with me at least, to this very day. I suppose it could be said that the apple didn't fall too far from the tree when it came to perfectionism yet I've spent my life being very hard on myself because of it.

Between replicating this work throughout store chains in various states and the floral arrangement classes that my father taught, I spent what should have been my summer vacations learning that art and co-instructing by his side. I expect that there might have been a blessing in there somewhere, perhaps my strong determination to succeed. I've never shied away from hard work, having learned this from standing beside our parents in every business venture they ever undertook. The downside for me is that I am a compulsive worker to this day. I never did learn how to relax and take enough time to smell the roses.

Looking back, I can see that my strong sense of obligation was pretty much borne out of fear of reprisal, yet my heart tells me that if hard work would have earned my mother's love and a sense of belonging, I'd have doubled my effort to make that happen. How many kids can honestly say that they'd have worked from morning to night to prove themselves worthy of their family's love? Some will take summer jobs for their own benefit and get to keep their earnings with no conditions attached to it. Others wouldn't have the foggiest idea what responsibility looks like and therefore, would be unable to stand on their own. So yes, I did yearn for freedom but feeling loved and secure would have meant so much more.

Lately, I've been listening to 60's music on the radio, hoping that it will help me to reconnect with my childhood. It really does work. A sad song seems to dredge up the traumatic memories that yearn to see the light of day, while upbeat songs are doing quite the opposite. I couldn't be more thrilled about that because it does my heart good to relive those rare times when my world felt happy and right! As I am able to evoke both good and tragic events, I hope to gain an adult perspective on those earlier years and share it with you in this book.

Allow me to share an event that meant a remarkable breakthrough for me, if only short-lived. The episode had its difficult elements to be sure but I do believe that I was blessed with an awesome miracle that will remain in my heart forever.

It happened during a winter break when the family had to hit the road for one of those working vacations. It was a long trip that ate up my entire break from school but it wasn't all work as it turned out. Our itinerary route had us stopping in Minnesota, where papa, *how I addressed my father at the time*, wanted to visit the gravesites of some of his relatives. When we arrived there, we were greeted by a pristine wonderland where everything was blanketed in clean, white snow. The trees were weighted with snow all the way down to the ground, as if they were inviting us to reach out and touch them so that we too might feel the presence of God's love in their branches.

When we reached the cemetery, we weren't prepared for the freezing temperature which seemed to grow colder with each step we took. The snow was deep, making it difficult to navigate, especially since I was not wearing winter boots and warm mittens.

By the time we were done visiting the gravesites, I had grown so cold I could not bear the pain of it any longer. The tears were freezing on my face as I ran back to the car, all the way causing my oxford shoes to fill up with snow and turning my stockings to ice. My feet were frozen and I know that I must have panicked, fearing I'd never be able to warm up again. By the time I reached the car I was in shock from the severe cold burning into my feet and legs. While my dad hurried to get the car warm, my mother held me tight, wrapping me inside her coat, while rubbing my feet in an effort to restore my circulation. By the time the heater began to blow hot air into the car, I was still so desperately cold that I held my legs and feet next to the heater, hoping for quick relief. Little did any of us know that this would cause extreme frost bite, requiring urgent medical attention.

Papa was so distraught that he might have been responsible for my condition, that he quickly pointed the car in the direction of Chicago, and didn't stop driving until we arrived at my uncle's home to get the medical help that I needed. My uncle was a doctor and would know exactly what to do. Papa's brother-in-law was a fine, upstanding physician, well known and prominent in the medical community, and yes, he knew exactly how to treat my frostbite, but it wasn't surprising that I swore off snow forever.

This was surely a special day to remember! In my heart, I knew that I had just experienced a miracle of love and belonging that I had never before known. My mommy had actually held me in her arms to warm and protect me, just as I had prayed to Heavenly God for when I was that little girl who was shoved outside to play in the freezing cold and snow. It was so ironic that it took a near tragedy to bring about that beautiful display of a mother's love for her child!

It was a treat for the senses when I first saw the lifestyle my relatives enjoyed. Papa's sister and brother-in-law lived in a huge estate home that even had an upstairs with an outside balcony and boasted so many features and comforts that the average person of that era could enjoy the daydreaming trip of a lifetime. It was a short visit yet long enough to show me how the other half lived.

When I began to feel better, my cousins suggested that jumping off the balcony into the deep snow below might be great fun. When I looked down from that high balcony and saw the massive snow bank below, I could feel the anticipation well up in me, causing me to feel brave enough to give it a try. Next, we donned warm winter clothing and gave it a go! Wow! That was a major thrill which I would never forget. I must have been nuts to try it, but I'm so glad that I did. After all, hadn't I been the one who had just sworn off snow forever?

My two cousins, J. Watson and I babbled and laughed so long into the night that my Uncle finally came down the stairs to tell us, "Okay kids, you've had your fun and now it's time to go to sleep!" Of course, that didn't work so he returned shortly after with what he called a mild sleeping pill, one each for us little chatterboxes. It wasn't but an hour before the last of us slipped into dreamland. I awoke to the sweet smell of hot chocolate and a huge breakfast being prepared in the kitchen. That sweet aroma was surely one of the highlights of our trip. If only life could always be this happy.

Next on our circuit was a visit to my papa's great aunt. It was a very long drive which meant spending a night in a motel. Once we'd settled in, mother and papa headed out to pick up dinner while I stayed back to look after J. Watson. I can't recall how long they were gone but I do remember that we romped and played together, having a good old time jumping on the beds. Just like a boy, J. Watson was a risk taker, jumping ever higher and having the time of his life. Then the worst possible thing happened. He bounced right off of the bed onto the floor and split his head wide open. Blood was pouring from the gash on his head and I wasn't sure how to stop it. I tried everything I could think of and it wasn't letting up. Panic and guilt set in as I realized I was in big trouble because it had happened on my watch. Thankfully, my parents returned a few minutes later and we rushed to the emergency room, where J.Watson received several stitches to close the wound.

Once we were back in our room, my mother flew into her usual tirade, attacking me where I was most vulnerable…my self-esteem. She ranted on and on about how ashamed she was of me and that I was worthless as a daughter and a sister. According to her, my only job had been to protect my younger brother for a short time and I couldn't even do that right, as if I wasn't feeling guilty enough already. I loved my brother but I was beginning to resent him deeply because of the many years of punishment that I had suffered on his behalf. I never spoke to him about it but after that incident, an emotional distance began to grow between us that would last for a very long time. I still regret that I didn't work it out with him when we were still children because many years had to pass before we were ever able to close that gap.

The next day, we arrived at papa's great-aun'ts house. As we approached her place, I have to admit that I was not impressed. The first thought that entered my mind was, "Oh nuts, another strange place! This must be a shanty home for sure!" We went inside and I immediately began searching for the bathroom. Surely every house has a bathroom but I sure couldn't find one in this house. When

I asked, my great aunt directed me to go outside. Well, that was a new one on me! I had never heard of such a thing so I asked her what a bathroom was doing outside. It was bitterly cold and the idea of using an outhouse wasn't anything I was prepared to do. So, no way was I going out there, preferring to stay in the house where it was warm.

Mother hated these things but kept her mouth shut for once which was a rare gesture of respect, coming from her. But oh, not me! I didn't hold back at all. I let it be known just how mortified I was that some creepy old wooden shack could possibly be used as a bathroom. The sharp sting of my mother's hand across my face let me know in no uncertain terms that she had no patience for my lack of manners, let alone my unfamiliarity with outdoor plumbing. There was little doubt that my aunt was wondering what was up with that. That was a short visit but one that taught me well—not everyone lives the high life such as we had enjoyed in Chicago.

After leaving my aunt's house, we spent our final night in a hotel and headed down the road toward home the next morning. J. Watson and I sat in the back seat, swapping our favorite memories from this trip, and laughing so hard that you might have thought we were little comedians, cracking up at our own jokes! Our Chicago balcony experience took first prize and a close follow up was the joke that we played on our cousins. When we had described our home back in Texas, I told them we had to ride our horse to the mailbox every day and they believed me. J. Watson went along with the joke, leading them to believe that we had a humongous property such as theirs, only ours was out in the country… *not true, we actually lived in the city!* Years later when they visited us, they couldn't wait to see our horses!

4

End of a Dream

Family Picture

My family moved back to Houston after my dad had recuperated. There, he opened a donut shop, named Poor Boy Donuts. I was about seven or eight when this photo was taken outside the store just before our Grand Opening celebration. It was my mother's idea to cram donuts into my mouth, insisting that it would make for good advertising for the business. How I detested that picture and I resented her intensely for using it for publicity purposes, especially when reporters published it in The Business Beat.

One of my fondest memories of that time was the patronage my father paid to the local orphanage, the same one J. Watson and I passed daily on our way back from school. Every morning, dad would prepare six dozen exclusively designed donuts for those little orphans, always hoping to put a smile on their little faces. As an act of kindness, he'd go that extra mile to be creative with his donut frosting which delighted those children to no end, perhaps even the high point in their day. We often got to go with dad on his orphanage deliveries. Looking back on those times, I learned what it meant to *Do unto others as you would have them do unto you.* We wanted to go there every day with my dad, but sometimes it was just too early in the morning for us.

The orphanage was a huge establishment for children who had no families to take care of them. I often wondered what life was like there—would it be a better place for me to live so that I could escape the beatings that I suffered at home? Was life lonely there? Wasn't there anyone in their lives who cared about them? I worried about those kids whose sadness was exposed in their eyes for all to see. Oh, but it was such a joy to see their eyes light up when we walked through that door with their heavenly treats. I even got to know some of these kids when we would stop and talk on our way home from school.

Yes, memories can be bittersweet at times yet when it was one of the good ones, I preferred to dwell on the 'sweet' part of it. At that time, the closest thing I had to a pet was, believe it or not, a duck. Let me tell you about my duck who I affectionately named Nuisance and why that name fit him to a tee. Every morning at dawn, Nuisance would park himself outside of my bedroom window, quacking so loud that he woke the entire neighborhood. It's safe to say that I was less than popular on my street. Each morning, mother would yell at me, "Get out there and feed him so he'll shut up!" So there I was, still in my PJ's and curlers, outside every morning feeding my duck. I'm sure that he didn't care a bit about that. He was hungry and I was his momma of sorts. I used to wonder if he was an orphan, secretly happy he chose me, of all people to love him.

That crazy little Nuisance followed me everywhere. He even followed me to school in the morning and there he'd be after school waiting to follow us home.

I could never figure out if he could actually tell the time or if he had an internal alarm clock that told him to 'go now'! Even when we locked him up, he still managed to break free and make his way to the school playground to wait for me like a faithful little puppy. Now if I could have taught him the days of the week, perhaps he would have let us sleep in on the weekends!

I used to believe that Nuisance was the reason I had any friends at all. Kids were fascinated with him and couldn't wait for the school bell to ring so that they could run outside to play with him. They loved to stroke his soft white feathers while he affectionately tucked his long neck into their armpits.

One Sunday morning, I awoke later than usual. My first thought was, "Where's Nuisance? Did he run away? Maybe he finally learned the days of the week and decided to let me sleep in." I ran outside to look for him and my heart broke when I found him. His head was stuck between the pond and the trench next to the pond tub which caused him to drown in the shallow water next to it.

I learned a lot about tragedy and grief that day as I cried over the loss of my special friend. I held him close to my body, hoping that my warmth would somehow revive him but it was not to be. Dad finally took him out of my arms and gently placed him into a special box he'd made. Then we held a special farewell service in his honor. Though I didn't get to say goodbye to him, I had to believe that he was in Heaven and knew that I would miss him forever.

How well I remember the fall mornings in Houston when the side-walks were so laden with morning dew that it was nearly impossible to walk on them. Between the dew and the morning traffic, we were not permitted to walk to school from the shop. That made my walk back with J. Watson all the more enjoyable when school was let out in the afternoon.

As luck would have it, it wasn't long before we ran into trouble on our return route from school. J. Watson, being on the slight side for his age, became a target for bullies and being the eldest, it was my responsibility to be his protector. How could I ever forget that burden—my mother never missed a chance to remind me that it was my obligation to keep him safe. She should have known that I didn't need to be reminded. I loved my little brother and I would never allow anyone to get between us, especially school-yard bullies!

Our walk from school to the shop was only a couple of blocks but you'd have thought it was a marathon, the way we sprinted to keep ahead of those brats. I did the best I could, but being only seven and eight, and far outweighed by our tormentors, a serious confrontation was inevitable. That day finally came and I did what I had to do. I plunged into the ditch ready for the rumble of my life. Yes, I fought them all and I won! This didn't make me the most popular girl with those boys, but at the age of eight, who cares! Being beaten by a girl wasn't exactly the kind of story those boys wanted to share with the other kids at school but they didn't let that stop them.

Wouldn't you know it; trouble greeted me the minute we got back to the shop that day. The dirt on my dress tipped off my mother that something suspicious had happened and she was none too pleased about it. I had been careful to clean up my brother to keep her from learning that we'd been in a squabble though I couldn't hide the stains on my dress. In those days, it was considered bad behavior for a girl to get into fights. Even though I had done it to protect J. Watson, I was still afraid that I might be punished anyway.

In the days to follow, mom became concerned about the scratches on J. Watson and why we were arriving later than usual back at the shop, so she decided to drive to school one afternoon to get the answers for herself. You can be sure that we weren't about to tell her. After all, he was her pride and joy and I'd surely be in trouble if she knew what was happening. Sure enough, she passed by that same ditch and caught the two of us fighting our little hearts out to fend off those nasty boys. She quickly stopped the car to help but sadly, that put an end to our walking for some time. I felt that my independence had been yanked out from under me but was grateful that at least the fights would stop and maybe, if I could catch a break, I wouldn't get into trouble with my mother for a while. Gee, how I missed my freedom but I couldn't argue that it was a relief to be free from those bullies. Mom reported those kids to the school office, which put a stop to the fighting once and for all. Finally, we were able to walk home again.

J. Watson and I did enjoy our afternoons at the donut shop. There we did our homework and waited on customers, for which we were rewarded with a freshly made donut with a big scoop of ice cream. Getting to and from school without incident also helped to maintain the peace. I'd have to say that this was one of my fondest memories, though there were precious few. At times like that, I truly felt like I was part of our family.

Waiting on customers was expected of us while I for one was only too proud to contribute to the success of our family business and our livelihood. My sense of self-worth soared at times like that because I felt like I belonged.

For me, waiting on customers was entertainment in itself. I made it a point to study people's eating habits that were usually normal but occasionally, unusual.

One customer stood out in my mind. Time after time, I'd watch him pour his coffee onto his saucer and slurp it up from there, and he wasn't quiet about it either. I had never seen such a thing! Oh my, hadn't we always been taught that "we do not slurp when we drink and we always eat with our mouth closed?" One day, after I'd bitten my tongue once too often, I decided that this man was due for a little lecture. Little did I know in my eight year old fervor, that I was committing a serious indiscretion by venting my revulsion for his rudeness.

I tried to hold back but my words escaped my mouth and blurted out for all to hear. "Sir, it is bad manners and impolite to slurp your coffee out of a saucer." Oh yes, you guessed right. I was back-handed right there for all to see! According to my mother, I had a knack for getting into trouble and deserved to be punished for my bad behavior.

Early one morning, just before sunrise, I was awakened from my sleep to the wailing sounds of our dog barking. I decided to get up and let him out if that's what he wanted. That's when I noticed heavy smoke billowing in from under the back door that led to the garage. Daddy had already left for the shop so I raced to my mother's room to wake her up. At first she yelled at me but once I was able explain about the smoke, she raced to the garage door and saw that the house was on fire. Mother quickly called the fire department, then joined J. Watson, our dog and I at the curb, where we felt safe. What a shock it was to watch our house burning. I shudder to think how much worse it might have been if our dog had not sounded the alarm in his own special way. He clearly understood that we were his family and did his duty in the only way he knew how.

A few days later the Fire Chief came to the shop and told mom and dad what caused the fire. He explained that it was a combustible fire, likely caused by the stuffing inside a doll. Hearing his words caused shivers to run up my spine. J. Watson and I had been playing with a doll that he got for Christmas one year. We were play acting and his doll was getting into trouble as usual. I recall shaking it before handing it to my brother to have a go at it too. Then J. Watson shook that doll so violently its head flew off. I panicked, knowing that I'd be blamed and punished as I always was. Not knowing what else to do, J. Watson tossed the doll up into the attic but it fell back down again. I threw it back up and that's where it stayed. Believing we were safe, not another word was spoken about it.

Oh my gosh, how I trembled as the Fire Chief's words rang loudly in my ears. That doll had caused the fire! I threw it up there and now our home was heavily damaged and it was all my fault!

To make matters worse, dad was sick from financial stress and the long hours that he had to put in at work. This time, I fully expected to suffer the beating of my life. I felt so guilty but we had only been playing and I just wanted to die. We never did confess yet I can assure you, she knew!

With the house so damaged, we were forced to move into the donut shop where we slept on cots and helped our dad out before and after school. As for my father, being captain at the helm of the donut shop with the long hours that he worked, it wasn't surprising that it took a major toll on his health. He suffered a major heart attack, forcing us to close the family business. That put an end to our walks to and from school and the sense of freedom we enjoyed, if only for those brief periods in our day.

Dad's heart attack brought unbearable stress upon our family. I suffered tremendous guilt because of the house fire, believing it to be my fault, however unintended. I was terrified that he would not recover at all. To complicate matters, my parents were fighting, often violently. Mother had to find work to support the family which caused a lot of friction between them. I tried to stay out their way, hoping to keep peace in the family. This was a difficult chapter in our lives which must have been all the more confusing for J. Watson who was too young to understand what was going on.

These were some of the memories that I struggled to unearth while writing this book. Guilt can have a powerful effect on childhood memory and mine was no exception. I remember keeping my special friends close to me and praying to God to put our family back together and while he was at it, to make us happy this time. I so wanted to be like other families who shared nothing but love and happiness. As a young child, I honestly believed that we were the only dysfunctional family on earth.

5

The Big Mistake

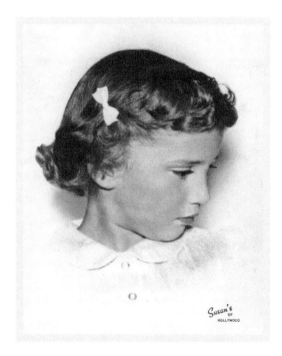

Mamie

Once again, my mother was forced to be the breadwinner in the family while our dad recovered from his heart attack. She took a sales representative position at a major toy manufacturer based out of New York, the toy mecca of the universe. Travelling her territory was an obligation that took her away from home for days at a time. Those were the only times that I felt safe, when Colena and my big brother Herb went out of their way to pamper me with affection.

J. Watson and I thought that this must be the best job ever, that we would be blessed with every new toy on the market. Well yes! I suppose that was true, at least for him, but I would not be so lucky!

You see, mom and dad had an opportunity to invest in the development of a promising new doll concept that would later become a superstar. My mother knew that I loved dolls and had no idea that this one would be the exception for me. The fact was this doll was not my type! She was just too tiny with ugly, hard, plastic features and I hated her. I was adamant that I wanted no part of her, perhaps because I had been denied the dolls that I had always wanted so badly—the pretty, soft ones and most of all, a teddy bear. According to my parents, my taste in dolls should have been an accurate gauge of what would be popular with little girls my age. And so they turned down the opportunity all because I preferred the soft and cuddly kind. This turned out to be a huge miscalculation on their part. For goodness sake, didn't I say that this doll went on to become a superstar? Had they simply heeded their own intuition, they would have found themselves on easy street financially.

Things went from bad to worse when my parents made another bad business decision. They invested what money they had into a warehouse and stocked it full of product from a major toy manufacturer to supply the retail stores in their territory. It was a bad decision because they jumped in head first without being able to afford insurance coverage for the building and contents. Late one evening, a fire marshal came to the house to inform our parents that the warehouse had caught fire and burned to the ground, destroying the entire inventory inside. This was financial devastation for my mother and father, leaving them in a state of sheer disbelief and despair.

Now it wasn't in my mother's nature to just 'suck it up' and accept the fact that they were the author of their own misfortune. It was more her style to find a scapegoat for the tragedy and in her mind, this is how she rationalized it. "If we had just invested into that doll, we'd be sitting pretty by now and not in financial ruin." So, this was how she justified it to herself. The fire was my fault!

I would be reminded of this cruel assault on my self-esteem every time she felt the need to lash out at someone. And lash out she did, with verbal and physical attacks that threatened to crush my spirit once and for all. Looking back at it all now, I wonder how I ever survived my childhood without a complete break from reality. Dad didn't even dare try to protect me. It was less stressful for him to just stay out of it.

I tried so hard to please her, yet she still flipped in and out of her dark moods and invariably, I would end up being her whipping post. It seemed that I had nowhere to turn, no one to lean on and no one to love me. These were the times that I turned to my imaginary friends. Where else could I go? What can I say about this special kind of friendship? They were loving, kind and loyal and knew exactly what I needed and was unable to find anywhere else, except for Colena and Herb when we could have some privacy to talk. My friends were my secret and I guarded their existence, for fear they would be found out and chased away. I don't know how I ever would have lived without them. Imaginary friends are a fairly common experience for small children and they tend to disappear as quickly as they came. Perhaps mine stayed with me much longer than they do for other children but then I likely needed them more.

Then one day, the unthinkable thing happened. I was playing in my room with my secret friends when my mother came in just as I was sharing my innermost secrets with them. At first, I didn't realize that she was listening in on our conversation. As you might expect, my punishment didn't come as a surprise to me and once again, I had to wear those ugly welts like merit badges, hidden from view as they always were and unbeknownst to everyone except my mother and I.

I so longed to have some privacy and own my own thoughts and dreams yet I couldn't escape my mother's intrusion into every recess of my mind. Sleep had been my only privacy up to that point but once my mother realized that I was a little sleep talker, she contrived a way to steal that from me too. She'd enter my room after I was sound asleep, sit on my bed and ask me about anything she wanted to know. I suppose that I must have heard her subconsciously because I 'spilled the beans' about all of my hopes and dreams, especially everything she wanted to know about my special friends. Once I understood what was happening, I felt so violated that I no longer felt safe to go asleep at night. I talked to my special friends about this and they already knew what my mother had been up to and urged me to keep on dreaming so that I would have something to look forward to. They'd be leaving soon and I needed to prepare myself for that.

Why oh why did God give me to a family that hated me so much? Was I such a bad child that He would always be mad at me? I had nowhere to escape to, no one to run to and no one to trust. Even running away wouldn't work. They'd just find and bring me back and my punishment would only get worse. If it had not been for the love of my older brother Herb and our nanny Colena, I would never have known what it felt like to be loved.

All of this was happening around the time I was in the fourth grade. I had a wonderful teacher named Mrs. Ethel Means. Kids would tease about her name, suggesting that it could only mean bad news. I can assure you that this was truly not the case. She was a caring and kind teacher, who taught us about loving all of God's creatures…well, most of them anyway. Mrs. Means kept a stuffed Koala Bear on her shelf that looked for all the world, like the one I had always yearned to own and love, except that mine would be a teddy bear. One day, I remember having an unexpected reaction to that bear. Resentment and anger welled up in me as I thought of this poor little guy having to die and get stuffed just so someone could put him on display. How could this possibly happen when I couldn't even have a toy one.

That was a turning point for me. I had definitely overreacted and she kept me after class to explain that this little koala was a gift that she cherished very much. She went on to explain that she was un-happy that this 'little guy' had to die. I felt so reassured when she told me that she keeps it with her at school to be sure that no one would ever hurt it again.

I suspected that Mrs. Means had other reasons for keeping me af-ter school. Her instinct had warned her that I was suffering great emotional trauma and she wanted to help by promising me that I have someone to turn to if I needed help. How I wanted to open up to her and tell her everything but I was afraid that she would let my mother know. Little did she realize that it was my mother who had been hurting me and not someone else as she had suspected. I begged her not to do that. In my heart, I knew that if she did call my mother, I wouldn't live long enough to draw another breath! I truly believed that.

It wasn't long after, that my teacher had occasion to coach my gym glass, substituting for my regular physical education teacher who was away that day. Mrs. Means came into the dressing room when I was changing into my gym suit and was horrified when she noticed the welts and scars on my hips and legs. I tried to run away from her but she didn't stop there. She pleaded with me passionately, "Oh my dear God! Child, what has happened to you?" I told her that I had fallen down the concrete steps outside of my house. I swore her to secrecy about that because I didn't want my mother to know that we had been talking about it. She seemed to understand my fears and reassured me by promising not to tell anyone about it. I knew in my heart that she was a kind and caring person who only wanted to help.

As we were getting close to the end of that school year, Mrs. Means tried again to get through to me. On that day, she asked me to stay after school to assist her with a school project. She said that she'd received permission from my mother and that she'd drive me home when we were done. Looking back, there really wasn't any project at all. Instead, we worked together re-organizing her classroom, hoping that this would make me feel important and give me a sense of purpose. After I relaxed, she asked me many personal questions, hoping to get me to open up about my problems. As young as I was, I knew better than to do that. I had learned all too well to keep my mouth shut.

Mrs. Means was such a good teacher and one who made a significant impression on my emotional development. She confided that she planned to quit teaching eventually and pursue her life-long dream of traveling around the world. She loved being a teacher but believed that it was just as important to pursue her dream. From that day onward, I vowed to myself that I would eventually have the kind of life I only knew in my dreams. All I had to do was believe that.

And so I continued to build a new life in my dreams that I did manage to keep secret from everyone else. It more or less went like this:

When I grow up, I will be the happiest person in the world! My beautiful house will be filled with laughter and peace and it won't hide any secrets at all. Someday, I will have a little girl of my own and I will always be her best friend. I will spoil her with love and give her everything that I have never had, especially my precious love. I will shower her with all of her favorite dolls and a cuddly teddy bear to sleep with at night so she will always feel safe. Oh, I forgot about the special play room that will belong to my little girl and no one else could share it with her, except her invisible friends. This room will be filled with doll shelves on every wall and she could play with them whenever she wanted.

After that, whenever life seemed unbearable, I had only to remember that dream to survive another day.

6

The Unexpected Fear

Mamie

Fifth grade was fairly uneventful except for the terrible fighting between our parents. Their arguments were very heated and usually turned violent, frightening the rest of us in the house. Either one of them could have started it but my mother was the instigator most of the time. We had never seen our father fight back before but quite simply, he had finally had his fill of her verbal abuse.

Thank God we were able to turn to Colena for comfort. She was always like a mother to us and we knew that we could count on her to be there no matter what. Some of my fondest memories were when Colena took care of us while my mother was traveling so much in her sales job. It was especially difficult when she'd return from the buying offices in New York. In fact, we could count on her to be crankier than usual and lashing out at everyone, especially papa and I. She never missed a beat when she repeatedly reminded me of the doll incident when I was younger and how it was my fault that she had to work so hard.

One day, Herb arrived home from school much earlier than usual, and touched off a chain of events that would change our lives forever. Upon entering the house, he interrupted a shocking scene that no child should ever have to witness. Mother was in the arms of another man, completely oblivious to the fact that her oldest son had just caught her in the act. As young as he was, Herb understood this to be a scandalous act and he demanded to know who this man was. That sent mother into a violent rage, and in retaliation, she picked up the telephone and smashed him in the head with it. This was an act that didn't end nicely at all. Mother wasted no time in having Herb shipped off to military school, leaving me alone and unprotected from her. I didn't know how I would ever bear life being able to lean on him. For Herb, being away from our mother was a welcome relief and a weight off of his young shoulders that should never have been there in the first place.

The fights between our parents continued to escalate until it became impossible to keep our family intact any longer, and so they made the difficult decision to end their marriage. Many matters needed to be settled, not the least of which was who would get the children. At one point, mother stood between my father and us kids, demanding that we choose who we wanted to live with—one or the other! For me, there was no question that I wanted to go with my papa where I knew that I would always be safe. It would be a welcome escape from her hateful verbal and physical abuse. As it turned out, I did leave with my Father and I have never forgotten her final words to me that day, when she screamed, "My attorney said that if you choose your Father you're not worth having as a daughter anyway- so good riddance to you."

Dad took us down that old familiar road to Angelton where we stayed in a large beach house in Freeport, owned by a close family friend. It wasn't long before 'peace and calm' moved in with us, promising to stay and keep us safe forever. At least, that was how I saw it at the time. I slept in a hammock by night and whiled away the hours by day, and walking the beaches with my dad. We even jigged for fish after dark under the stars, although I was a bit squeamish about what creatures might crawl across my feet as we stood in the black sea water. It was so much fun even though I never did catch any fish. Each night, I would lie in my hammock while the swishing sounds of the surf and the gentle breeze in my hair would lull me off to dreamland, so much like a lullaby.

My dear reader, didn't I tell you that there were some good times in my life? Well, this brief getaway with my papa had to be the best one ever! But it didn't last. That delightful symphony of sensations that seemed almost too good to be true turned out to be just that.

Wouldn't you know it! My father missed home, and felt that he could make another go of it with my mother. He decided to settle for 'the devil he knew rather than the one he didn't'! I begged him to stay away and let us live our lives alone but my pleas fell on deaf ears. We moved back home and since Herb was away, I tried to find solace in my friends, who would only spend time with me at school because they were uncomfortable around my mother. They were anxious to help but all they could do was reassure me that it would all work itself out someday, that I would eventually escape and my nightmare would finally be over. Little did I know that my dad would put us through this distress over and over again. This was to become our new norm—leaving just to return again and again.

Why they stayed together is so beyond my comprehension that no explanation could possibly make any sense to me. Surely it wasn't for love! What was love anyway? It was never an emotion that could be found within the four walls of our home, at least not by Herb and I. Any love that was in her heart was reserved for J. Watson, a fact of life that bred intense jealousy and resentment toward him. I would later understand how this resentment would be the root cause of many more issues in my life.

Upon returning home, my worst fears were realized. I was not to get away with choosing to leave with my father. For that, I paid a dreadfully high price. The beatings came in rapid succession to the extent that I was terrified to be in the same room with her.

Now, what I'm about to tell you is both frightening and unthinkable. Earlier today, a sad song that spoke of child abuse came on the radio and I have to say, it shook me to my very core. Immediately, a memory that I had been struggling to resurrect, sprang to life, just as clearly as if I were watching a movie in vivid technicolor. I was caught in the middle of it, forced to relive every traumatic emotion that I endured the day it actually happened. This movie was cast with my mother, Colena and I. I'm not surprised that Colena was there because mother so loved to terrorize me in her presence, as though she needed to have an audience that was powerless to stop her.

Scene #1 – mother tells Mamie to fill the glass coffee pot with water and put it on the stove to boil. *The pot was one of those old fashioned glass kinds usually found in restaurants of the day.*

Scene #2 – mother instructs Mamie to remove the boiling pot of water from the stove.

Scene #3 – Colena panics and yells at mother, "Miss Sara, don't let my baby take that pot off the stove – it's too hot!"

Scene #4 – mother ordered Mamie to remove the pot and the unthinkable happens. The bottom of the pot falls out, and splashes scalding hot water onto both of Mamie's legs.

And of course, it all happened that way. As I recalled it, I could actually hear myself screaming from the pain in my legs which felt like burning coals eating into my flesh. Colena scooped me up and raced toward the bathroom to put me into the tub to run cold water onto my legs. All the while, Colena was shouting at my mother, "I told you not to let my baby pick up that hot pot! Now get in here right now and help me put her legs in some ice." When mother didn't respond, Colena screamed at her, "Miss Sara, I'll tell Mr. Jack if you don't get in here right now and help her!" That worked because together they packed my body in ice while I sobbed in pain.

I know that Colena saved my life that day. I can't believe that mother would have lifted a finger to help me if it hadn't been for Colena taking control of the reins in that emergency situation. She continued to treat my burns with special salves to keep me from scarring. She even had a salve to heal my broken heart, as only she knew how.

Her salve was called love, and it sounded like this, "Child, yuz got to get up, brush yuzself off and start all over again. Colena loves you my baby!"

There were no witnesses to this event, other than Colena. Herb was away at military school and J. Watson had gone to Angelton with dad on a short business trip. Mother warned me to keep my mouth shut about this 'accident' and to reassure anyone who asked, that I'd been clumsy and fell with that pot of hot water and burned myself. This must have been one of those memories which I'd suppressed and now I could see it all so clearly. And to think, all it took was the power of that sad song to remind me of this horrific event that had been buried so long.

It wasn't long before summer was upon us again. This year, the four of us traveled to San Angelo, Texas where mom and dad had business to transact. Herb was still away at military school and I missed him terribly. I had hoped he would reclaim some sense of well-being but he was happiest to be away from home as much as possible. How I longed to see my cousins again in Chicago but this was not Chicago. This trip was all business with a very tight schedule.

One evening, J. Watson and I accompanied our parents to a large warehouse. Mother instructed me to take J. Watson for a walk around the building while they conducted their business with the owner and buyer. In one area, we came upon some workers who were laying a new floor. Adjacent to that was where toys were stored. Oh my, what a treat that was! There seemed to be an endless variety of the latest toys to come on the market. In our excitement, we forgot to pay attention to our surroundings and exactly where we had wandered into, or how to get back. We could always worry about that later.

Suddenly, without any warning, the building exploded all around us. We were caught up in multiple fires caused by bursting hair spray canisters and the detonation of ammunition from the adjacent storage area. Out of sheer panic, I grabbed J. Watson's hand and began running, looking for a fast way out. It was impossible to see beyond the growing wall of flames and smoke that surrounded us and we had to cover our faces with our clothing to avoid inhaling the acrid smelling fumes. We were both screaming, praying that our voices would be heard so that someone would come and rescue us. Just then, I heard the voice that answered my prayer. It said, "Get down on the floor and crawl as fast as you can. Just follow my voice to the door!" It was my dad, who was trying frantically to rescue us from this burning inferno. When we finally reached the door, we quickly stood up and ran with our hands clutched together toward the safety of the outside air.

J. Watson and I emerged first, followed by our dad. Mother was right there and ran towards my younger brother and grasped his small body close to hers. Our lungs were filled with smoke and we were each trying desperately to breathe but there was our mother, thanking the good Lord that her last born was still alive. I watched as she held J.Watson and doubted that it would ever be my turn. I wondered if my dad felt the same way.

As we learned later, the workers had run out of the non-flammable contact they needed to adhere the flooring to the sub-floor, so they used a flammable glue instead. It only took a small spark to ignite it.

God was our parent that tragic night and I was to ask him many times in my prayers why I had been spared, if only to live out my life in loneliness and despair.

7

My First Crush

At long last, fifth grade was behind me, with only one more year to complete at Red Elementary School. I had a good feeling that this year would be my best yet. After all, I had Junior High to look forward to next year when I hoped to begin a new and much happier chapter in my life, and mostly grown up.

Here I was, all of 10 years old, and the youngest in my class. I had started school at age five instead of the usual starting age of six and was far more mature than other girls my age. Yes, I was a big girl now and looking forward to enjoying more privileges that were appropriate for my age group. The first good thing was my new school schedule which got me out of the house earlier than ever. It was a blessing to have more time to myself away from home and out from under that dismal black cloud which hung over my head whenever I was under the same roof as my mother.

All in all, I was enjoying a bit more freedom. In some ways, I found that to be empowering, a concept that was entirely new to me. I even became more inventive about staying on the good side of my mother. In the past two years, J. Watson and I were able to earn an allowance by selling little items that she picked up on her sales travels such as wooden pins for blouses and dresses and toy tops that spin. Now, being in the sixth grade, we were able to spend our money at the Village Theatre, watching afternoon matinees. We always saved our popcorn money and went next door to buy mother a special gift before she came to pick us up. We were only able to afford little junk items but it felt good to put her in a better mood. She was always so happy when we presented her with our little gifts and for me, it was a way to keep the peace for at least that day and occasionally, for a few days at a time.

Now, nothing was perfect in my life... not by a long shot. There were many anxious moments for me in grade 6, especially when it came to getting along with my school mates. I'll never forget having to wear my ugly eyeglasses to school when other kids who needed them were sporting the latest fashion trend. In general, it was not popular to be wearing eye glasses at all but if yours were in style, somehow it was more acceptable and a sign of class. Such were the 'class wars' that I had to endure back in the day, especially since my Mother forbade me to wear what I felt most comfortable in. As I said, my glasses could only be described as ugly and kids had a great time poking fun at me in the hallways when I wore them. It wasn't uncommon to find me fighting back when I was being picked on, usually because of one thing or another that I was forced to wear to school.

Difficult or not, I must confess that school was still the safest place for me to be. The time I spent with my friends more than compensated for any unhappy experiences I was going through at home. In some ways I was enjoying more freedom but I was never completely out of my mother's sights at times when she had it in for me. Mother grounded me a lot that year although I was getting to be good at staying out of her way.

I continued to keep my dream of escape alive and well. After all, who could blame me for wanting a better future and home life? I attached a lot of importance to school as being the doorway to an exciting future, without fully understanding that a child my age didn't have a whole lot of control over her destiny. What I did know is that I had to keep my dreams alive and blossoming in order to survive if I were to have any chance at all of making them come true. How I longed for a time when I no longer had to shoulder the blame for every misfortune that befell my family and for every misdeed that J. Watson ever committed.

Talking about dreams, I hadn't even considered how it might feel to experience my first attraction to a boy until it suddenly and unexpectedly happened to me. It sent me completely off balance and I was dominated by this new emotion…well, let's call it a 'first crush' because that's exactly what it was! I had met a young boy named Ben and I had a best girlfriend for the first time whose name was Diane. Golly, I had such a huge crush on this boy! He was so good looking and treated me just like a princess. It wasn't long before he was inviting me to share lunch with him and confiding his deepest secrets to me. It turned out that his home life was pretty much the same as mine. Diane and I became fast friends and shared our most daring thoughts and dreams with each other. Who else but a best friend would know and understand how it felt to feel this way about a boy. These times where always shared at school because my Mother would not permit me to have a social life that she could not control. This was my friendship and my time and I was determined to make the most of it.

As in life, things do change and good things are not meant to last forever. I had a reality check when I discovered that Ben was just as fickle as the other boys and even a so called 'best friend' might not remain loyal for long either. This was happening to me all at once and turning my whole world upside down. I no longer trusted anyone and it took quite a while for the sadness to pass.

I was feeling pretty much like an outcast when I met a new friend who would help me to rebuild my confidence. She was an adventurous soul who encouraged me to take a few chances and make things happen for me, instead of to me. Together, we changed our 'big heartbreaks' into the 'big get even' and all we had to do was go out of our way to make our 'exes' jealous. By the end of that year, we got our wish. Our 'first crushes' began to pursue us again by inviting us to the sixth grade dance. I had bounced back, proving that I was capable of taking some measure of control over my life. Oh, what an exhilarating experience that was!

My younger brother and I were as different as night and day. J. Watson was known as a 'real looker' among the girls, the heartbreaker that girls fell for from a very young age. It wasn't unusual for him to turn the heads of many girls at the same time, all attributed to his groovy charm and good looks. How I longed to be more like him— sweet, popular and outgoing, all of which I was not. I had serious trust issues that invariably would interfere with my social life.

The school dance was fast approaching and now it was only a week away, just before Christmas break. My mother had agreed that I could have a party back at the house after the dance. Can you imagine how excited I was when she took me shopping to buy a new dress? I could hardly believe that I was going to have my first formal gown! How WOW was that or so I thought. Sadly enough, what my mother had in mind was atrocious as far as I was concerned but I had no choice. Her mind was made up. Not only that, she dragged me to the beauty salon and insisted on having my hair cut short and permed. I was mortified! How in the heck was I ever going to look pretty when I had a head full of frizzy curls and a silly dress when my friends all had long hair with soft shiny curls and the latest in fashion for our age?

I should have guessed that it was all too good to be true. Why couldn't my mother just accept the fact that this was my first dance, the kind that sweet memories are supposed to be made of? I had every right to be happy but now I'd be the laughing stock when the other girls were wearing pretty dresses and trendy hairstyles. A deep sadness overtook me and I no longer believed that I had a chance to ever enjoy a normal life. Now I had to go to that stupid dance and make a spectacle of myself! Thank you very much Mother! It was going to be her way or no way at all, proving just how unimportant my feelings were.

My worst nightmare was realized when we arrived at the dance. Just as I expected, the other girls were all wearing sweet satin dresses, looking all sophisticated and pretty. Mother had decided that I should look like a demure 'southern belle' and my dress certainly filled that bill. It was white with many tiers of lacy ruffles, something that you might see on a little flower girl at a wedding. As if that wasn't bad enough, she made me wear a hoop skirt under my dress, which resembled something that you might see in a southern movie. "My friends, have you ever tried to sit down when you're wearing a hoop skirt under your gown? I didn't think so." Oh my goodness, you can't imagine how I felt when my dress flung into the air above my head. I'm sure there was a technique for keeping that dreadful hoop under control but it was too late for that now. Little did I know it would be J. Watson who would come to my rescue. Like a true little hero, he rushed over and stood in front of me as a shield so no one else could see. How had he become this dashing little gentleman at such a young age? If you asked him about it now, I'm sure that he would have no idea just how much I loved him that day.

It didn't take long before Ben lost patience with my embarrassing hoop behavior and decided to abandon me for a prettier girl. Once again, my younger brother came to my rescue and stuck by me for the rest of the dance and at the after party, my friend Burns danced with me so that I would not feel alone in my own home.

I was so humiliated by this chain of events that I gave up any notion of having a boyfriend or attending dances at least until I was in Junior High. I learned that it was pointless to even try when my own Mother, who always looked so beautiful, would go so far out of her way to make me look bad.

Mother and I fought a lot that year but for some reason, I wasn't suffering much physical abuse. Instead, she resorted to a severe form of mental abuse and that was just as bad. I was older now and couldn't expect my invisible friends to show up anymore, but I can't tell you how much I missed them. Colena was away with her family and Herb was still away at military school and so I had no one to turn to for moral support. To stay out of trouble with my Mother, I took my Dad's direction and tried to stay out of her way. He suggested that if I gave up on boys until I was older, she might allow me to learn a musical instrument. I really wanted to believe that because I so badly wanted to take piano lessons. The answer I got was that they couldn't afford to buy a piano or lessons but who knows, maybe next year.

My saving grace was my firm resolve to keep my dreams alive. I was determined that I would make that great escape someday but for now, I was content to believe that a whole new world would open up for me at Junior High. My parents were planning a summer road trip and I crossed my fingers that it would go quickly so that my brave new world could begin. I had to believe that God would finally hear my prayers and open up a whole new world of love and happiness for me. I reminded myself every day…one more year and my new life at Junior High will be all mine!

8

Sara's Revenge

Yippee! Junior High, here I come! At long last, my big day had arrived and I was beside myself with anticipation as I contemplated a brand new social life. Being more grown up, I was ready for added privileges and the kind of equality with my friends that I had only been able to dream about before. I was close to being a teenager now and I had no intention of looking back ever again.

At my dream school, I had more trouble than ever keeping my head out of the clouds. I imagined all sorts of wonderful things, such as love, happiness and good fortune. I knew that I was looking at my life through rose-colored glasses but conjuring up those amazing images felt so good I wasn't about to stop for anybody. My typical daydreams went something like this.

I'm walking down a paved street in a small country town. At times, I see myself floating around on billowy clouds much like a ballerina. Later, I reach for the stars where I know all my dreams will come true.

Now, to be completely realistic, I knew I couldn't make every dream come true, but I could surely make the most of my opportunities. The old saying, 'the bigger they are, the harder they fall' brought me back down to earth with a thud when my mother decided to interfere again with my fashion and grooming choices.

Here's how it started. I was ecstatic about dad taking me to buy my new school clothes. I knew in my heart he would understand how important it was for me to be on a level playing field at school. Shopping with him was definitely a treat long overdue. Among other things, he bought my first straight skirt, a gorgeous white one and a pair of heels. Now the new me had finally arrived and I could be one of the girls. No more tomboy with *Phyllis Diller* curls that frizzed like *Curly Kate* every time it rained!

Then came the thud! The very first thing my mother did when she saw me in my new skirt and heels was force me to go back to the store and be fitted for a girdle, a long lined bra with stays and some nylon hose. That was the only way she would allow me to keep what dad had bought for me. Her words still sting to this day. "You're too fat! No one wants to see a girl who isn't properly under-clothed." I could always count on Mother to do everything possible to make me unattractive to boys.

Next came my hair! This time she had it cut really short with more curls added, making me look for all the world to see, like a *Shirley Temple* doll. I could just picture those springy curls popping off… boing, boing, boing! How could she do that to me? In short order she had transformed me into a complete nerd, and destroyed my dream of being just like all the other girls at school. I would be an outcast again and I couldn't do anything to stop it.

Remember those ugly undergarments? I had to obey Mother and wear them but I tried to hide them in the change room when pre-paring for gym. When that didn't work, I became the laughing stock at school. Oh, I forgot to tell you Mother grounded me from wearing my new skirt and only allowed me to wear it to church where all the girls dressed up in white.

School was good for the most part and I tried to fit in with my friends. There was one issue, however, that hurt me more than I can say. A couple of the girls refused to eat lunch with me because of my ridiculous hair and clothing which didn't conform to the group. I had told them how much I loved my new white skirt but I was forbidden to wear it to school. Well, one of these so-called friends dared me to wear it so I would look more like them. I so wanted to be 'cool' so I took the dare. The next day, I took my skirt to school and changed in the girl's washroom. I knew my mother was working late that night and I would have time to beat her home to change. Or, so I thought, before the disaster…

So, picture this! There I was sitting at my desk, feeling 'oh so cool' in my trendy white skirt when I suddenly felt all wet and blood soaked. This could only mean one thing. Oh, dear God, how could this happen! Of all things, why would God allow my first menstrual cycle to happen in class when I was wearing a white skirt? This was a double whammy because now I'd be a huge joke at school and would also have to face my mother with a lot of explaining to do unless I could wash out the blood stain without her finding out about it. Can you imagine how freaked out I was when the boys and girls in my class began laughing and making fun of me? Before I knew it, I was down on the dirty floor duking it out with as many kids as I could handle!

The next thing I knew, we were all sent to the principal's office where our parents were called to come and pick us up. I knew my dad would be disappointed and angry with me but I was thankful mother was working late. Imagine my panic when it was mother who showed up instead of dad. She had come home from work earlier than planned and had answered the call from the principal. Oh man, couldn't anything ever go right for me? I just couldn't catch a break anywhere. As she approached me, all I could see was black smoke shooting out of her eyes and I just knew I was in for the beating of my life.

I wanted desperately to tell the principal my mother was going to beat me when we got home but I knew I might not survive her rage if I did. No one else knew what my mother was capable of and the abuse Herb and I had been subjected to for nearly our entire lives. I began to shake uncontrollably as I followed her to the car. In looking back, I know if Herb had been home, he would have protected me but I shiver to think of what she might have done to him if he had helped me. I often wondered if he knew how much safer he was to be living away from home at military school.

Oh, my dear friends, my heart is racing as I share this with you. My memory has returned with full intensity as I relive the horror of what my mother did to me that day. I must tell it and put it to rest forever or I fear I'll never be healed.

When we arrived home from school, mother immediately ordered dad to leave the house and take J. Watson with him. That left Colena at home but then, wasn't that just how she liked it? I knew all too well that my mother took sick pleasure out of having a witness to my beatings. Colena came rushing immediately when she heard me screaming hysterically but she was powerless to stop her.

Mother ripped the clothes from my body and dragged me by the hair into the bathroom where she shoved me into the bath and turned on the cold water full force. She waited until the water ran icy cold and then held me down until it took my breath away. As I surfaced, I screamed in pain, promising to be good and never do anything again to make her angry. I begged her to stop but she was just getting started. Out came the wire coat hanger that she beat me with until my hips were spurting blood. I could literally feel the jagged edges of the hanger tearing the flesh from my body. Through it all, I could hear Colena yelling, "Miss Sara, Miss Sara, please don't hit my baby no more!" It was utterly hopeless because Colena's pleas fell on deaf ears. Mother's rage knew no bounds and she seemed powerless to stop herself.

When I crumpled to the floor of the tub, she turned on the hot water and made me sit in it until my skin was so red it looked and felt as though I had been severely scorched in the blazing sun. I believe I went into deep shock but I vaguely remember Colena still begging her to stop, "Miss Sara, if you don't stop beating my baby, I'll call the police and tell Mr. Jack and all your friends what yuz done to my baby all these years. Yuz a mean woman and God will punish you one day." That ended it because the only thing my mother feared was being found out for the sadistic monster she was.

She had beaten me before with a wire coat hanger but never so brutally as she did this time. It was as though she intentionally measured each strike to my bare body to ensure I would suffer the maximum amount of pain and damage. My brother, Herb, had witnessed it on earlier occasions but Mother was always careful not to allow anyone else to be around. Just like Colena, Herb was helpless to stop her. To this day, he tells me it hurt him more deeply than I'll ever know that he was unable to protect me from her madness.

Dad stayed away with John for the weekend at the beach house and Mother confined me to my bed. That was okay with me because I was in too much pain to move anyway. If I'd had my way, I would never have to look at her evil face again. For that entire weekend, I was not allowed to leave my room unless I had to use the bathroom, a place that I now associated with terror. Late at night while mother was sleeping, Colena would sneak food into my room. It was so comforting to have her there at my bedside as she fed me and told me how much she loved me and that she would never allow Miss Sara to hurt me like that again. Even at my young age, I understood that Colena needed her job to support her family and so it would be a difficult promise to keep.

I did a lot of thinking that weekend. One thing I knew for sure was that I would never again crave love from my mother. I was done with her and as far as I was concerned, I no longer wanted to be her daughter. I mean, what was love anyway? Certainly mother had no idea when it was anyone except J. Watson. Her obsession with him was still a mystery to me because love was not an emotion that she knew anything about. Perhaps it was because my sweet brother was her last born and she felt compelled to spare him.

A strange thing happened when I was alone in my room. My imaginary friends returned and stayed beside me until it was time to leave my bed and return to school. I can't tell you how healing that was because I thought they had left for good now that I was older. They encouraged me to hold onto my dreams, for the day would surely come when I would live in a beautiful mansion like my uncle's place in Chicago, have a wonderful husband who loves me unconditionally, and someday birth a precious baby who would only know the beautiful kind of love that a mother is supposed to give to all of her children.

While I felt a fierce determination to have that life someday, doubts kept creeping into my reality. I mean, "Who was I kidding anyway?" My life was a living hell and I had no way of knowing how to escape it. Instead, I vowed that I would take control of my future one way or the other. Yes, this was the year that I would finally be free!

Oh, I know I swore off ever needing her love again. That was just my way of retaliating after a severe beating and it did help me to recover. Sure enough though, whenever I found myself in the throes of despair, I would came running back for more, needing to believe that maybe this time, she would love me back.

Sadly, the only time she ever showed any affection toward me was in a public setting and only then, when it would benefit her social status or when in the company of her business associates.

9

Reflections

Mother, Herb and Mamie

What ever happened to loving and protecting me?

Dad and Mamie

I've often wondered about the heart of an abusive personality. Is cruelty caused by a mental illness or can it be a learned behavior? Was the abuser mistreated as a child? Why can't love reside there instead of that mysterious darkness that induces extreme rage and contempt toward others, especially toward one's own family? I suppose that any or all of the above reasons can account for it but what of the woman who was born and raised into a loving family and provided with the finest things that life could possibly offer? And finally, how is it possible for an abuser to love one of her children so deeply while feeling extreme hatred toward the others, using them as whipping posts every time she needed to take her frustration out on someone? I knew that one size did not fit all but in mother's case, she fit all of them. So many questions but so few answers...

And what about victim behaviour? Why is it that victims of abuse turn their suffering inward, always trying to figure out what they did wrong and trying to fix it in order to earn love and affection? These were the questions that I wrestled with as I struggled to understand why Herb and I were unable to connect in a loving way with our mother. I was older now and I needed answers yet there was no one to turn to.

Even our father knew enough to stay out of her way when she was in one of her many black moods. I used to think that mother's excessive doting on J. Watson was unnatural. He was adorable and sweet yet seemed unable to hold him accountable for any of his childish pranks or misbehavior. It was easier for her to deflect that blame onto Herb or I. It always hurt so badly to see her shower so much attention on him when we were in company or in front of her business associates while Herb and I stood back and watched like obedient little puppies.

Forgive me if I dwell on these reflections a bit longer. It helps me a great deal when I'm in the throes of searching for a memory that's been eluding me and while I am trying to make sense of things after all of these years. These are the times that I think most about Herb, who's been helping me, even to this day, to sort out this maze of events that were my so-called life.

Looking back, I wondered if there was ever a time when mother felt any love for me. Did she love me when I was a baby? J. Watson was only eleven months younger than I. Did she stop loving me when he was born? Surely to God, there are answers to these questions, though trying to find them was much like banging my head against the wall. Oh yes, God knew what was wrong with my mother but I was just too young to understand.

When I think about Herb, I recall missing him with all my heart. He was loved dearly by our grandparents but in her own cruel way, mother used him as a pawn. Our grandparents were extremely well off and had raised their daughter in great style... *country club and the whole nine yards.* This lifestyle was to cease abruptly when she married my dad, who was forever struggling to make ends meet. But leave it to mother who was a genius when it came to getting her own way. If she wanted a new dress or to play the 'Mrs. with style' she simply told her parents they could see Herb, their grandson, but it would cost them anywhere from a hundred to a thousand dollars for the weekend. It's hard to believe, but she was happy to sell him off if the price was right.

Through the time that Herb was away at military school, I missed him with a passion. How I needed to have him by my side to protect me and to be my confidante. But who wouldn't understand why he wanted to stay as far away as possible to escape our abusive mother? Not only had she hurt him physically but her emotional abuse had done even more damage to his spirit. Being held up for ransom and his painful memory of walking in on her sordid affair had damaged his spirit in such a way, that his only hope of recovering was by maintaining a safe distance from home

I, on the other hand was stuck in this pathetic place called home where love was never in the forecast. Even after a torturous beating, mother expected me to act as though everything was normal but the dark secrets between us continued to fray away at my heart until I thought that it would harden and finally break apart into a million pieces. Oh how I prayed that God would take me away or better yet, take mother away and drop her off on some distant planet. At times like this, I missed Herb the most, as though my heart had been ripped out and fed to her demons

I'm reminded of a time that took place at the Willow Meadows Country Club in the Houston area. This was where mother would don her 'high society' hat and play up to the 'see and be seen' jet-setting crowd. We went there often as children and knew exactly how she expected us to act, perfect in every way. There was to be no hint that we were not financially well off and relied on our grandparent's reputation for being in good standing in the community. The only way that we even knew what that looked like was from the way that our grandparents lived. Don't get me wrong; while they lived the high life, they were loving and kind, unlike the spoiled brat that was their daughter.

On this particular occasion, I was still recovering from mother's vengeful attack in the bathtub and the welts and scabs on my body were still fresh and angry looking. She hadn't yet had the opportunity to use her classic excuse about my so-called clumsiness. Instead, she had bought me a new bathing suit with a ruffled skirt in an attempt to hide the damage. She further instructed me to stay out of the pool, to sit in a lounge chair and pretend that all was well and right with my world. So there I sat, next to the 'queen of the snobs' sipping away at my *Shirley Temple* while I watched my brother doing high dives into the cool refreshing water.

Oh, how I wanted to join J. Watson who also pleaded with our mother to let me go in and swim with him. It was so hot and sultry outside so I prayed that she would say yes. Other mothers were insisting that she allow me to go in as well. She finally relented. While my new suit covered my most severe wounds on my back, hips and buttocks, it didn't completely cover the marks on my upper legs. When asked what had happened to me, she gave her stock answer that I was just a 'clumsy girl' and laughed it off. I was never surprised by her excuses but always shocked when they believed her.

It became blatantly clear to me that escaping was the only answer; otherwise, I would never live to see my next birthday. Now, more than ever, I knew that it was time to make some viable, elaborate plans. Without Herb to help me, I had to do it on my own. I could no longer cope with the terror and the constant fear that I may not recover from the next assault.

My first attempt came when I accompanied my father on a business trip to Arizona for a long weekend. While there, I met his business associate's son and got to know him fairly well. He seemed to know that I was troubled and sensed the truth about my unhappiness. It was as though the opportunity just dropped out of nowhere into my lap. He offered to meet up with me at a gas station if I could make the break and help me to enter a shelter with people he knew.

I felt so bad about doing this to my dad but I was desperate to make my break. So, while he was resting, I snuck out of the hotel and ran as fast as I could, not once looking back to check whether he had seen me or not. But sadly, he did, and when he caught me, we high-tailed it for home. He was so angry with me, more because he knew that his own life would be a living hell if I had gotten away.

I can't begin to describe just how petrified I was to walk through that door to face my mother. I knew this could very well be the last day of my life, if past experience was any example. My punishments had become increasingly harsh and my poor body just couldn't take anymore, much less my broken spirit. As predicted, she waited until J. Watson had left for school and dad had driven off to work. My mind was racing. What could she possibly do to me that she hasn't done already?

They were no sooner out the door, when she grabbed me by the hair and flung me to the floor. She then began kicking me in the head and face and I grabbed the closest pillow to protect myself. That was a big mistake because she shoved that pillow into my face so forcefully that I feared I was going to smother. I couldn't break free and when I was about ready to pass out, Colena came home and began screaming those all too familiar words, "Miss Sara, Miss Sara, please don't hit my baby no more. Yuz got to stop, Miss Sara, please!" In my heart, I was screaming to God. "Please get me out of here now!" I knew I had to get out or die!

Mother's violence was escalating rapidly and I had no idea how I could possibly endure yet another beating. After each incident, I felt in my heart that this must surely be the last, that the next one might be a homicide. I wondered if she even knew that there were boundaries and she had crossed them all. I was defeated beyond all imagination and had no confidence in myself whatsoever that I could manage a successful escape on my own. It didn't stop! It never stopped! I kept on surviving and I had no idea how! I was so lost and I wanted to disappear.

Another year went by with no break in the routine. I kept wondering how it was that my baby brother never questioned why I was continually grounded, always in trouble with mother and was clumsy so much of the time. At one point, I even wondered if he was being abused as well. What happened when I was being sent out of the house? Just the thought of that sends shivers up my spine! Then I reminded myself that from all outward signs, J. Watson was still getting all of the loving attention that any child could ever dream of. Whatever he wanted, mother made sure that he got it.

I was heartbroken when mother bought a set of drums and lessons for J. Watson, simply because he asked for them. Hadn't I been begging for years for piano and voice lessons because I felt music so intensely in my soul? I would get lost so deeply in *Bach* or *Beethoven*, that I wished to stay in that special place forever. But no, I was told the family could not afford a piano and J. Watson was the only one in the family who could carry a note anyway. The fact was, both J. Watson and I loved music but his wish was always mother's command. It all happened on one of our working summer vacations, when we were traveling through a little town in Montana. We stopped at a bar for some lunch and refreshment and the most wonderful band was playing. We were both swept up in the music but J. Watson was especially fascinated with the drums and the showmanship of the drummer, which was entertainment in itself. This is when he decided that drums would be the instrument of his choice. And so his wish was her command.

According to my mother, she had always wanted to play the organ but for some reason, was never gifted with one. That was strange because she had been the proverbial 'spoiled child' who always got what she wanted from her parents. So it really came as no surprise when she decided that I would take organ lessons. This was a done deal that came along with the instruction to, "Just learn it! If you want lessons so badly, this is your chance!" Should I have been happy about it? It was keyboarding after all but 'close' did not satisfy me. I so resented the fact that I had no choice in the matter and I hated that nasty instructor who was always so impatient and making me feel stupid, causing me to give up after only a few lessons. My failure didn't sit well with my mother but this was one time that I rebelled and got away with it. From her point of view, this would be the last of my begging for something that she had no intention of giving to me. Even today, I still long to sing but it's too late to train my voice.

As I continue to reflect, I flashed back to a time when mother would use J. Watson and I as her personal servants. She loved to entertain friends and business associates and therefore, it was imperative that she leave the lasting impression of good taste and manners, befitting her position in life. I was accustomed to being her little slave in the kitchen but now that J. Watson was getting older, he was assigned kitchen duty alongside of me. I carried the 'lion's share' of the work because after all, 'I was a girl' and was expected to remember that.

A typical dinner party was a nightmare. I waited on her guests hand and foot, responding to their every need... *bring me a fresh napkin please, refill my glass please, show me where the ladies room is please...* *well, you get the picture.* I lived in sheer panic that I would make a mistake and pay for it later after her guests were gone. Before the night was over, I spent hours on end restoring the kitchen to its usual tidy condition. I hand washed dishes for what seemed like hours, being careful to return them to their assigned locations without breaking any of my mother's favorite pieces of dinner or glass ware. Those were the times when a dishwasher would have been a blessing.

The more she expected of me, the more I found myself shaking from sheer dread that I would perform less than perfectly and embarrass her in front of her guests. Why in Heaven's name couldn't my dad or J. Watson see what was going on before their very eyes? Could they not sense my fear when I was even in the same room as my mother? I knew that my dad chose to look the other way when he suspected that I was being victimized but surely J. Watson was old enough to sense that something was just not right about what went on in our home and that I wasn't that accident prone after all. I can only guess that they too, were afraid to speak up.

As I delve deep into my memory cave, searching for a lighthearted story to end this chapter, this one just popped out at me. One day, while our parents were out, J. Watson noticed a gargantuan spider crawling across the ceiling. Being the man of the house for all of a minute, he ran to get his BB gun to shoot it right between the eyes! Well, he really wasn't a bad shot, if you're trying to kill a chandelier, that is! Okay, that's the end of the comical part. When our parents came home, mother decided that since I was the oldest, I must have provoked him into this odd behavior. Without thinking, I retaliated. "Is there nothing I can ever not be blamed for doing?" The result was predictable but it must have been a good day because it was just a beating of the 'average' kind.

By now, you know that nothing happened in an 'average' way with our mother.

Typically, her abuse was so severe that I feared for my very life. She was capable of anything, acts that today would end with her children being taken away from her. If she could sell Herb off to his grandparents, was there anything that she wouldn't do to me? Sometimes, I wondered if she was even sane!

10

Hopeless

Mamie, Herb and J. Watson
Could a normal life with love ever be ours?

By now, I was taking classes in French and Biology science where I met a young man who really got my attention. I could tell that he liked me and we would get to know each other so much better. His name was Jimmy and he was a real looker with dark hair and smoldering brown eyes that could cast a spell on most anyone. Oh yes, I knew I was in love this time! Jimmy even wrote poetry for me and we ate lunch together every day. In no time, we became inseparable. Oh my goodness, I can't tell you how much it meant to me to have a boy love me back just for myself. This was surely an emotion that I had never known.

And just as suddenly, I made a fatal mistake! Like always, my happiness was too good to be true. I had shared my deepest secrets with him and didn't hold back when it came to my mother's abuse. After all, he was my sweetheart and surely I could trust him with my life.

Imagine my surprise when Jimmy invited me to come to dinner to meet his family. I was thrilled, feeling that my life was changing for the better as I had hoped. I had no sooner relaxed into our meal when Jimmy began to tell my story of abuse to his parents. For a brief moment, I actually felt as though I was being welcomed into this wonderful family. Boy, was I naïve! Right out of the blue, his mother stood up and faced me with a cold stare. "This is nonsense," she said! "It has to be crazy. No mother would ever treat her children like that. Now dear, I think you'd better leave."

My heart sank. Was there no one who I could trust in this entire world? All I could feel was shock and despair. Just when I thought I could finally trust someone, I got sold out again. Now, I was frozen and defeated, terrified to go home in case my mother would find out. I so wanted to give up but took another chance that God might hear my prayer this time. "Please God, if you want to help me, take me to a safe place where I'll never feel this fear again.

Please don't make me go home. I just can't do this anymore." With Herb and Colena both away, J. Watson at his friend's house for the weekend and Dad being away for a week with Daddy Sam on business, I knew that I'd have to face my mother alone.

I roamed around for what seemed like hours, crying hysterically and wondering how I was going to survive. Tears were still streaming down my face when I found myself crouched in a corner of the outside wall at my grandmother's house. I had found a ride all the way across town only to find that no one was home. Would God help me this time? Would grandma come home soon and let me stay with her?

I didn't have to wait long. Maybe God sent that police car that stopped at the end of the driveway. The officer got out and asked me if I was in trouble or was I lost. Yes, I was positive that God had sent him and that I finally found someone to trust with my story. Out of desperation, I blurted out what had been happening to me all of these years and how petrified I was to go home. I hoped he would understand and report my mother to the authorities so I could finally be taken away to live with another family. What he said next totally crushed what little spirit I had left. He told me, "It's not nice to lie about your parents that way. Your mother called us and reported you missing." That was when I took the long ride to Hell!

As it happened, Jimmy's mother had called mine, and let her know about the stories I'd been telling behind her back. Of course, she didn't believe a word I'd said. She just thought my mother needed to know about it. My mother immediately called the police and told them that I had run away because I'd been rejected by my boyfriend. And it got much worse than that! She twisted the knife in the most hurtful way when she added that this so-called boy didn't even like me, that I'd likely slept with him and that she intended to take me to her doctor friend the next day to be examined.

This was not even possible. I was a virgin and knew nothing about sex whatsoever. Jimmy could have assured his parents of that had he not been so afraid to stand up for me. No thanks to my mother, I would be labeled a 'bad girl' and the butt of jokes among my friends. She had finally ruined my life.

Being true to her word, she dragged me off to see the doctor the next day. I hoped that her plan would backfire when I had to remove my clothes, revealing all of the bruises and scars on my body. I was hopeful when the doctor noticed and asked my mother to explain how they got there. Once again, she delivered an award winning performance with her usual explanation about extreme clumsiness. It was unbelievable—she had gotten away with it again! Next, I was forced to have a pelvic exam which turned out to be so painful, I screamed out in protest. The doctor handled me so roughly that I bled profusely, soaking the white paper on the examination table. I'll never forget the look on that doctor's face when he said that it didn't appear I had ever been sexually active.

We went home where I went to my bed, wishing that I could just go to sleep and never wake up. I became obsessed with death and thought about it most of the time. I had no one and nowhere left to turn. Nothing was worth it to me anymore and hope was something that I only used to know. I can't begin to explain how shame became the final nail in my coffin. My soul was shattered and I hadn't even done anything wrong.

I would continue to struggle, knowing beyond all doubt, that my life would keep worsening. Nothing ever abated. Fear became my second name while mother defeated all the odds as she became even more vile than ever before. After all, she had shown a side of herself that no child should ever see. She was indeed the monster who had driven me to the very edge, not being sure whether to jump or to give in to the false hope that things could actually get better.

I cried myself to sleep for many nights until I was finally able to feel some hope again. Dreaming began anew and I was able to sooth myself with the illusion of a loving and safe lifestyle much like my cousins enjoyed in Chicago. I vowed that if I could somehow manage to survive this ordeal, I would become the best person I could possibly be. Looking back, I think this was my way of getting the 'dirt' off that Mother had so cruelly painted me with.

Hopelessness was becoming my new mindset while I continued to search for new ways to escape from reality. This is where music came in. Little did *Bach* and *Beethoven* know that they played a significant role in healing my soul but I swear that it happened just that way. Classical music would take me to a private world that I could truly call my own, but I worried that if mother found out, she would do her level best to destroy that too. As with everything else that I cherished, she would always find a way to snatch it away from me, as though she resented the fact that I could feel love for anything at all.

I think that my teacher, Mrs. Genz, was tuned into the way that music seemed to sweep me away. When listening, I would become intense, almost inward as I concentrated on every note. At the end of class one day, she asked me to stay. My first reaction was that I must have done something wrong because she had never asked me to stay before. I needn't have worried. She simply wanted to know what the music was trying to tell me. What was I hearing that was so intense and private that I transported into a world that didn't include another living soul? I didn't quite know what to tell her for fear that I would say too much.

Mrs. Genz seemed to detect my discomfort and decided not to push me too hard. Instead, she asked if it would be possible for me to help her out after school for about an hour in the classroom. When I got home, I nervously approached my mother, hoping that she'd say yes. She did agree but not without breaking another little piece of my heart with her hurtful words. "If it'll give you some work to do and keep you out of my hair for a while, then go ahead, but don't expect me to give you a ride home." It didn't matter. She said yes and that's all I cared about.

The next day, I remained after school to help Mrs. Genz. We worked but still managed to talk a lot. After I had relaxed, she decided to play *Beethoven's 5th Symphony*, a dark piece that was composed in the 1700's. When she turned up the sound, I immediately felt myself floating into that space and time as though I were at a live concert, except that my concert was a complete visualization of women wearing long gowns at a grand ball. I'd been swept back in time to a wonderful era that I never wanted to leave. Then just as suddenly, I was snapped back to reality and my former despair.

My first thought was about Herb. I missed him so badly but I understood that he was at peace and needed to stay away. I longed to share my passion for music with him and wondered if he would have experienced these same emotions but I would never know. As tears of sadness overtook me, Mrs. Genz turned to me and placed her hand on my shoulder, hoping to reassure me that everything would be alright. She had never seen a reaction such as mine but she knew that something was terribly wrong. I wanted so badly to confide in her but it just wasn't possible. I had learned all too well that no one would ever believe me, that my mother's word would always prevail over mine, destroying every shred of credibility that I might have had.

It was getting late now and it was time for me to leave. On my way out the door, Mrs. Genz presented me with the *Beethoven* album for my very own. I couldn't hide my delight that such a precious gift was now all mine. I carried it close to my heart as I ran all the way home to show everyone.

I had missed supper so I went straight to my room and played that music loud enough for everyone to hear. What was I thinking? Had I not learned anything from past experience? I should have known that Mother would destroy anything that made me happy. Easily disturbed, she barged into my room and caught me waltzing around in my own little world. She ripped that record from my player and broke it in half. Then she smashed it onto the floor where it broke into hundreds of pieces. She justified it by proclaiming that this music was from the dark side and she could not allow it to taint me. As I sat on the floor staring at my broken record, she passed by me on the way out and slapped me in the head while telling me to get it cleaned up and get to bed. I must have moved too slowly because she returned soon after to pummel me some more.

When I returned to school after the weekend, I wasn't sure how to handle a conversation with Mrs. Genz. We stayed after school and she attempted to draw me out by trying to engage in conversation. Then she introduced me to *Johann Strauss*. Oh my goodness, I had never before heard anything as beautiful as *The Viennese Waltz*. Just as I had with *Beethoven*, I was propelled into a different space where everything was a fairyland of dance and multi-colored flowers.

When it ended, Mrs. Genz asked me how I enjoyed the *Beethoven* album that she had given to me. I was afraid to tell her the truth and so I explained that I'd fallen when I was running home and it had broken. At first, she wasn't pleased and it hurt so badly that I was unable to tell her the truth. Her reaction was completely justified. "You get a gift and destroy it before the day is even out? What kind of foolishness is that?"

I began to weep, knowing that I'd hurt her but when she reached over to touch my face, I recoiled in horror. "Oh my God child, what are you so afraid of?" she uttered with tears in her eyes. I reacted without restraint. "Please don't hit me! Oh I'm so sorry. I thought you were going to strike me in the face and it's the only part of me that isn't hurting!" I knew I'd said too much and that would mean more trouble for me. Just then, she put her arms around me and quietly reassured me, "Never give up sweet girl. Someday you'll be free. I promise I will never tell."

I knew that I was suffering from a severe form of trauma, much like shell shock. I could no longer restrain myself when anyone moved too close to me. My hands would fly up to protect my face, betraying my every attempt to keep my secrets from ever seeing the light. I was so utterly broken that I would rather have died than to ever go home again.

How was it that Herb, Colena and I were the only ones who knew the insanity that was my life? My father failed me miserably by always looking the other way when I was suffering at my mother's hands. Had he stood up to her from the beginning, he may have been able to keep her more under control. In many ways, J. Watson had been shielded from the cold hard truth but I'd be willing to bet that lately, his good life was not so good anymore. I may have been jealous of him but it wasn't his fault that our mother hated Herb and I. He too was a victim only he just didn't know it at the time.

After all that mother had put me through, I still wanted her love more than life itself. And that was the paradox—it was this need for her love that kept me alive.

11

The Grand Scheme of Things

II

Mother was never known to be the rational one in the family but every so often, she went way too far. She began to act strangely and I couldn't help but wonder what she was up to. She was making frequent trips to the local supermarket and dropping odd remarks to my dad about a guy who worked there, named Robert. I was curious about her odd behavior though didn't dare ask

She seemed to have an unusual interest in his welfare. I wasn't sure if it was a physical attraction for Robert or if her concern about him was genuine. About nine months into the year, she decided to move him into our house. Imagine how mortified I was when she actually gave him a twin bed in my room. I had no interest whatsoever in sharing the privacy of my room with a stranger, yet alone a strange guy! Naturally, mother didn't ask me if I minded. The deed was done and I had nothing to say about it. She told my father it was because he was homeless, but trustworthy and hard working.

Oh my dear God, what was she doing to me now! The next thing I knew, she was demanding that I be 'extra friendly and loving' whatever that meant yet I knew nothing about him or even wanted to, much less with someone that my mother chose for me. Well, it got worse...*much worse in fact.* I was to treat him as though he was my first real boyfriend! She warned me within an inch of my life. "Do not screw this up! This is your final chance to prove to me that you're worthy enough to find your way into my good graces!"

I had to admit that all of this gave me an idea for an escape plan. I'd been wanting to run away since I was very young yet never had the wherewithal to make it happen. Now if I could only convince mother that I was going along with her plan or at least being cooperative, I had half a chance to finally break free. Robert hadn't been hiding the fact that he wanted to take this arrangement to the next level and quickly at that. So what if he wasn't the light of my life. I knew what would happen to me if I didn't at least convince mother I was going along with her plan.

In my heart of hearts, Jimmy was my true love but mother had forbidden me to be friends with him or even to speak of him. We'd been reassigned as lab partners that year and it was emotionally painful for me to be near him, knowing that we could never be more than that.

I kept stalling with Robert yet couldn't help but realize that he just might be my ticket out of there. At the very least, I had to show that I was interested enough to make him feel loved. So I kissed him! My mother must have thought that I was slow and became a little more graphic about her expectations. She demanded that I 'take care of him' because it would be awfully painful for him to have 'blue balls'...*whatever that meant!* I detected the underlying threat but this time, dug in my heels. I would fake it, but no way was I going to be her 'whatever' and I meant it.

To make matters worse, it got back to me that mother was telling people I was a whore and had slept with Robert, forcing her to put him out of our house. It seemed that her plan had failed so she created the lie to back up her original story, that she had taken pity on this poor guy and brought him into our home for a better life, and lo and behold, she had caught him fooling around with her daughter. She was such a deceitful liar but I was glad to see him gone. I couldn't help but wonder why she had gone to all of this trouble. Why had she hatched this scheme in the first place?

The fighting at home became a daily nightmare in my family. There was never any peace for any of us except J. Watson. Beatings were not limited to Herb and I anymore but had actually extended to my dad. He was the stronger of the two physically but that didn't stop her from trying. Believe me, there were horrible things that went on between the two of them that I can't even bring myself to go into here—perhaps later. It seemed as though her violence was becoming a full time occupation with our only chance at survival being to stay as far out of her path as we were able. I never knew when her attacks might become deadly and change our lives forever.

Herb is and always was my only reason for sticking it out. Even then, there were times that I had tried unsuccessfully to escape. When he was home, I at least had someone to turn to and confide in but when he was away, I felt abandoned and vulnerable to her abuse. Thankfully for him, he would soon find his own salvation and would no longer be subjected to the pain I was going through.

My older brother always knew how to make me feel special and all the more so because he knew how desperately I needed to matter to someone. The highlight of my life that year was a special gift from him… a gold bangle bracelet with two roses on top. I cherished that bracelet like it was sent by an angel and even today, I take it out from time to time and hold it to my heart, remembering that he was the only one in my family who ever put me first.

I would soon be sixteen and was more desperate than ever to get away from my mother once and for all. I had rediscovered Daniel, the most incredible young man to ever exist. He was handsome, polished, hardworking and he loved me! That was a winning combination that was so right for me. I was now old enough to realize what I wanted out of life and I sincerely believed that he was Mr. Right. I had known him for several years, having met him on one of mother's sales calls but it wasn't until recently that I saw him in this wonderful new light. As you might expect, there was no way mother would ever allow me to be with him. It was more in her interest to keep me as her servant and whipping post with no chance for happiness now or ever. I had to keep him a closely guarded secret or risk losing him like I had Jimmy.

You might remind me that I thought I'd been in love before. Well, I was much more mature now and this was no ordinary teenage crush. It was deeper and felt so much like the 'real thing' that I'd go to the wall to find my way to him. In the long, lonely nights, I'd dream of him and plan new ways to get out of this 'nightmare, knowing that it needed to be elaborate or it wouldn't work. So I devised a scheme that I felt my mother might go along with.

It was 1962, the year of the Seattle World Fair. Mother had been planning to take us there and to Disneyland. Gosh, I had always wanted to go to Disneyland. Yes, I would make my escape from there. With my plan in place, I contented myself knowing I'd soon be free. It would also give me some quality time with J. Watson as a memory to carry with me.

As it turned out, our Disneyland trip didn't work out as planned but I wouldn't give up. Colena was with me in spirit this entire trip and begged me to call her whenever I could sneak away from my family. I managed to call her twice and let her know how much I loved her and missed her.

Colena knew I wanted to bolt. Before we left, she pleaded with me not to do it. "Child, I'z got a bad feelin' about this and I knowz that your mama is watchin'. She'll kill yuz if she catches yuz runnin' for sho!" She loved me like a mother should love her child. I knew enough to listen to her and decided to stay put. She promised to help me make a break when I returned home. Looking back, no one ever knew that her love for us children was so strong, she'd put herself on the line to help me with my biggest plan of all.

Colena had been right. We were no sooner through the park gates when mother grabbed me by the hair at the back of my head and warned me. "Do not try anything! I'm watching your every move!" I told her that I had to use the bathroom. Instead of waiting, she followed me right into the stall... as if I could escape from there! When I flushed the toilet, she again grabbed me by the hair and shoved my head into the wall, warning me in her most menacing tone. "I know you want to run but you'd better think twice before you try it!" I think I literally saw stars and my head was throbbing with pain. I thought I was going to black out but I managed to get a grip on the door to catch my bearings. When we left the stall, I was crying hysterically while mother was busy telling anyone who would listen that I'd fallen and hit my head.

I was terrified and filled with resentment toward her at the same time. I swore that I was going to enjoy this trip and there wasn't going to be anything that she could possibly do to ruin it for me. I wasn't going to allow her to break my spirit. I kept reminding myself of Colena's loving words, "Get you'self up, dust you'self off and start all over again!" In truth, I was tired of all of the falling down and starting all over again but I swore that I was going to enjoy this vacation one way or the other. Disneyland was for happy families and I was determined to experience the joy of it, even if it meant pretending that my mother and I were having the time of our lives together.

All in all, I did have great fun on the rides, especially one called 'It's a Small World' which featured dolls from around the world. Each country's doll was life size and bedecked in full cultural costume. I concentrated on the wonderful magic that was all around me, allowing me to shut out the horror of what had happened as we had entered the gates to this fairy tale wonderland.

On the final day, mother dogged my every move, as though she expected me to make a run for it at any moment. Any happiness I had experienced dissipated immediately, knowing that I was returning to that hell hole called home. I calmed my fears by keeping that delightful ride and Colena's promise close to my heart, needing to believe that my escape was just around the corner. Colena had witnessed far too many beatings, so many that she too had become afraid for my life.

Back home again, I was back at the drawing board to plan my next move. I needed a foolproof master plan if I was ever to be with my true love, Daniel. I had met a boy at school who was just as unhappy at home as I was so I recruited him and my new plot began to hatch. He became the focus of my escape plan yet had no idea that it would change his life forever. His name was Anthony, a sad but very nice teenager. The plan was logical, self-serving for both of us and caused us to shudder with excitement that we may actually get away with it all. To keep it as simple as possible, I told him nothing about Daniel.

So what was this grand plan anyway? As I was considering the merits of eloping, a better plan had come to mind. Why not convince our parents we were madly in love and if they didn't allow us to be married, we'd run away over and over until they finally agreed? It only made sense since neither of us was wanted anyway. Wonder of wonders, both of our parents agreed and in no time, we were on the road to Mexico for a quickie wedding. They even gave us a wedding shower of sorts along the way. We planned to find an apartment of our own when we returned to Texas. Now, the way the law worked in Texas, a person at the age of sixteen was legally considered to be an adult with all of the privileges. That meant that we would both be free on my sixteenth birthday. Of course, we both vowed to make the most of it until then.

I thought we shared the same strategy but would soon find out that Anthony had a different motive. We started our lives together in a small apartment, each sleeping in different rooms, expecting this marriage to last only a few weeks.

Naturally, I didn't contemplate a sexual relationship with him...*it just wasn't in the plan.* I could only focus on my upcoming freedom...one that would spearhead a whole new future.

Now, freedom is a seven letter word but deception is nine and quite another as I was to learn all too quickly. My eyes had been set firmly on the prize, only taking into account a means to an end. When I reflect back, I hadn't given much consideration to Anthony's needs and was panic stricken to learn that he actually had other ideas in mind. What a disaster! YIKES! Anthony decided that our life together was better than anything either of us had ever experienced. He wanted to consummate our marriage just like any other married couple and he wanted to do it now! That night was long and exhausting as I rejected his persistent and unwanted advances. A cold chill set in between us which threatened to derail our plan right out of the gate. Eventually he fell asleep but I knew it was time to do some damage control.

How was I going to hang on for another two weeks until I turned sixteen? This was not fair. He was breaking the rules! We had planned to file for divorce after my birthday and, as an adult, I'd be free of both my parents and Anthony once and for all. I tried to hang in but it became so bad over the next week, I had no choice but to end it with him...*he simply had to go!* I was a virgin and there was no way that my first time was going to be with someone I had no feelings for.

That night, I literally dreamed of a way to be rid of Anthony. If he would not leave on his own, then I'd just have to get rid of him myself. My first concern was getting away with it without being caught and being forced to go back home. Incredibly, my dream laid out the entire plan before my eyes and I knew exactly what I had to do... *or so I thought!*

Ammonia? "Yes, you heard right." I would put ammonia on Anthony's toothbrush! It had to work, so I did the deed and sat back, waiting for him to head for the bathroom. I was unbelievably cool about it until the cold reality set in and I began to hyperventilate. I raced into the bathroom before him and with my entire body shaking and tears running down my cheeks, I grabbed his toothbrush and threw it into the toilet. I had conjured up a picture of myself being led off to prison. I never did like the color orange or even stripes for that matter.

After an intense argument with Anthony, we decided to talk to my parents to convince them that our marriage was bad...*very bad!* We rushed over to their house. By the time we got there, Anthony was so angry, he put his fist through the sheet rock wall of my mother's bedroom instead of swinging at me. I never thought I'd be begging my parents to let me stay there, but at least I knew the devil who lived under that roof. I didn't know Anthony's anger or what he was capable of and didn't plan on finding out. If you guessed that I didn't get any sympathy there, you'd be right. My Mother snarled out at me. "You made your bed so now you'll have to lie in it." Somehow I thought they would understand since their own marriage was such a joke.

I returned to the apartment, hoping that I could stall for more time, at least until I turned sixteen. At last, it was the day before my birthday and I went out and filed for divorce early in the morning. What I really needed to do was 'give my head a shake' and think before I acted! I should have waited one more day and I would have been home free. As it turned out, my divorce notice was published in the local newspaper that very evening and as luck would have it, my parents read it. All I could think was, "Oh my God, now what am I going to do!"

Our parents wasted no time, getting us to a small town just over the border into Mexico. This time, they paid off an official to annul and backdate a marriage license so that neither Anthony or I would be deemed to be adults at sixteen as we had planned. Although I don't recall the exact legalities related to the age of sixteen, it was clear that my plans had been foiled once again.

And so I returned home, with the full realization that I had come oh so close to freedom. If I were to succeed once and for all, I would not be so foolish as to drag a third party into it. So far, all of my escape plans had been fairly well thought out but didn't take into account the unexpected things that could and did derail them. From now on, I would examine every detail before acting, especially any plan that had come to me in a dream, for goodness sake!

Mother resumed her watch over my every move. She made my life a living hell on earth...*no telephone calls and no friends were allowed to visit.* Quite literally, I was under house arrest with little or no chance to think, much less breathe without sensing her shadow at my back. I would contrive what I thought were elaborate schemes and it never failed, one way or another she would find out about them. Was I so transparent that she could read me like a book? And then it came to me.

Jumpin' johosephats! I was talking in my sleep again...*mother asked and I boldly answered.* She knew every detail before I even had a chance to make the first move. How dare she! Had she no shame? She had done it before and now she was doing it again. This time

I let her have it, at least in my thoughts. "Okay then! Enough is enough! This time you aren't going to get away with it!" I vowed there would be no more night time revelations because I would beat her at her own game, even if I had to stay awake all night to do it! At the very least, all I had to do was wait until she had fallen asleep each night.

Oh no! She would not learn of my grandest plan of all!

12

Escape Plans Complicated by Homework!

I was only sixteen when I concluded that my life would never improve or ever be tolerable if I remained at home. This was not living but barely existing with little or nothing to hold onto but hope and prayer. I had to get out once and for all and I knew, beyond all doubt, my next plan must be my final one. I could no longer distinguish between the need to escape sixteen long years of physical and mental abuse, save my sanity or even to save my very life. I suspect that it was all three. I felt certain that another failed attempt might very well put me over the edge. I was barely hanging on as it was. My only chance at survival was to get back to the drawing board and get planning again. This time, I was fortunate enough to have an accomplice who was older and wiser than I, and who had the wherewithal to make it work.

Now that Daniel and I had fallen love, I truly believed that someone was on my side and wasn't going to leave me when the going got tough. No longer would I depend upon my dreams to offer up naive escape plans but he and I would plan my departure from that hell hole called home, with the utmost maturity as a team.

How I loved Daniel! I loved his pure, honest and compassionate heart and the beautiful devotion that he expressed toward me...*like nothing I'd ever known!*

"Oh, and did I tell you that he was a 'real hottie' and six foot six? Oh yes, I think I did!" He was the total package and made me feel like I'd 'died and gone to Heaven!' Now, keep in mind that I was barely sixteen and knew very little about true love but I can tell you that I felt the most incredible sense of peace and security when he was near. I just knew in my heart of hearts that he was my destiny. Daniel assured me that he would take whatever risks were necessary to rescue me once and for all.

In the meantime, I had to bear my mother's cruelty for a bit longer before I'd be free to begin a new life of true love and happiness. I asked myself then and still do today, why I had never physically retaliated in an attempt to overpower her during a beating. In retrospect, perhaps I should have but I never wanted to learn the 'art of abuse' for fear that it would become my nature, a disposition that I despised with everything that was in me. Then I would remember that my mother had extreme psychological power over me. She knew just how badly I needed her love and how to manipulate me into submission in order to 'earn' it. One of her favorite reprisals was, "You're a no good, stupid waste of a daughter. If you ever want to get into my good graces, you'll do things my way!" Well, her way invariably left deep welts and bruises on my small-framed body and emotional scars that would never heal in my heart and soul.

One evening, mother came in my room to ask me why I wasn't doing my homework and I replied that I was stuck on a problem and was trying to work it out. She then accused me of lying and day dreaming. It didn't take much imagination to see what was coming next, so I apologized quickly, hoping that we could end it there without my being punished or grounded. True to form though, it didn't end there. She grabbed me by the hair and shoved my head back, as though I couldn't hear her words unless I was forced to stare into her madness, eye to eye. I pleaded with her to stop. "Oh please mom, don't hit me. I promise to get my work done." Instead, she slapped me repeatedly across the face while yanking my head back and forth until I thought my neck would break. Her rage still not spent, she shrieked more venom in my face. "If you've got enough time to daydream, then here's another assignment for you!" Then she ripped the clothes from my closet and dresser drawers, leaving them in a heap on my bedroom floor. Finally, she instructed me that I was to put them back where they belonged and do my homework before I'd be allowed to sleep.

As I sobbed, she warned me to be quiet and not wake up my younger brother, J. Watson. He had no clue that mother was perpetrating these night time attacks and she surely didn't want to disillusion him about her true character. Just for once, I wished that he would walk into the middle of it and see her for what she really was, an evil monster of the sickest kind. I loved my brothers but could not reach out to either of them...*Herb was away and J. Watson was too close to mother to see her in a realistic light.*

My sleep that night was so fragile that by morning, I could barely get out of bed. Not only was I sleep deprived, but my entire body ached and I was chilled to the bone. I'm sure that stress had a lot to do with it. I went back to bed to get warm for a few minutes, hoping that would help. Instead, I fell back to sleep and awoke to the sound of the front door shutting as Dad left with J. Watson to drop him off at school. That would be my usual warning that some 'mommy and me' time was about to explode in my face.

Like clockwork, mother entered my room and dragged me out of bed, screaming at me all the while. "Get out of that bed you useless piece of trash! What did I ever do to deserve a lazy little brat like you?" All I could do was beg her to let me stay home that day. "Please mommy, I'm sick! Please don't hurt me!" My next words just fell out of my mouth without warning and certainly with no forethought. "Maybe you and daddy and I can talk about why you hate me so much and then we can fix it!"

Now, I've had more beatings than I can count but never before had I seen mother's rage so intense. Her reaction was quick and sharp and before I even had a chance to recoil, she hit me with a bone chilling warning. "You will never talk to your dad about any of this! I promise, you really won't want to know me if you do! DO YOU UNDERSTAND?" Then she yanked my head back with one hand and struck me in the throat with the other. I lost my breath immediately and couldn't seem to recover. My throat swelled up and no amount of gasping would allow me to catch my breath. For the first time ever, she seemed to realize that she may have gone too far. Panic stricken, she ran to get an ice pack to place on my throat. Then she applied a menthol type of salve, in the hope that it would return my breathing to normal. She even tried steam in another unsuccessful bid to help me to breathe freely again. She must have realized that I was going to survive because she didn't hit on me again that day. She just left me alone and closed my door, not realizing that it would take me several more hours before I would be able to breathe normally again. When dad came back, she told him I seemed to have a bad case of the flu and would be staying in my room for the day to keep me from infecting the entire household.

Colena arrived about midday and when she saw me, she just knew. How could she not? She had been witnessing these assaults from the time I was four and felt my emotional despair just as deeply as any amount of physical harm my mother had ever inflicted upon me. I raised my finger to my lips as I cautioned her to whisper. I feared for both Colena's and my dad's safety. Mother had warned me that harm could come to them if I ever revealed the truth about what had happened. Colena held me close to her heart and I understood that she would put an end to it all if she only knew how. Her good intentions meant just as much to me because they were borne out of love.

I may have slept but the next thing I knew, Colena was sitting next to me with a glass of horrible tasting whiskey and insisted that I drink it all. It was warm and there may have been something soothing in it, perhaps honey, to make it go down more easily. I slept again, and when I awoke, Colena was still sitting by my side in a rocking chair as though she had not moved from my room all day. I was still unable to speak and my throat remained sore and swollen. In a raspy voice, I managed to let her know how peaceful it was to have her near. "Colena, I love you so much. Why can't mommy be just like you?"

I stayed home from school for the next few days while my mother actually left me alone for a change. You can bet that an apology never escaped her lips. This last time was different though. I honestly believe Mother realized for the first time that I might have died at her hands and feared what the consequences would have been if I had.

I could no longer afford to crave the security of my mother's love. It was never going to happen. She simply had no use for me, other than to serve her warped needs. Colena and I both understood that I might not get out alive if mother lost control again. This was a cruel and heartbreaking realization but there was no longer any hope left in me. I had to break out to save my sanity and hoped that Colena could live up to her promise to help me this time. She even reminded me in her own sweet way, "Child, yuz gotta get out of here while yuz can!"

I had so many unanswered questions. If she hated me so much, why would she try so hard to keep me around? I was never able to break the strangle hold that she had over me. Would I forever be that little girl who was left out in the cold, praying for dear God to help me? I could only find comfort in my daydreams where I could visualize Daniel stealing me away to a lifetime of happiness.

If you concluded that my mother was a control freak, then you'd probably be right. When it came to my needs, she was completely devoid of compassion. All she cared about was keeping me under her thumb and crushing my spirit. Who else would be her whipping post when she needed to vent her pent up frustrations? She was so inside my head, it was as though she were reading a statement of confession. But looking for a rational explanation for her behavior was an exercise in futility. There wasn't one. The woman was insane.

You'll recall that I'd been trying to escape since the age of eight but of late, my planning was much more guarded. I wanted so badly to know how she knew what my every move would be before I made it. Was she still invading my sleep at night? Worse yet, was she a mind reader? Or was I simply being paranoid? No matter what I planned or thought, Mother was still finding out and I had to get to the bottom of it.

I ruled out sleep talking. There were no longer any middle of the night beatings to give her away, yet she still knew every detail of my escape plans. So how then? The only person I had confided in was Daniel. My heart began to pound at the very thought. "Oh God, please don't let it be Daniel!" I ruled him out just as quickly. Surely, he would have no reason to lead me on and then sell me out to my Mother. But wait! Hadn't he and Mother been friendly for years through their employment? "Oh Father God, please don't let it be my Daniel! There has to be another way. Could someone else have heard me talk in my sleep?" Then, for a split moment, I wondered if it could possibly be the only one who had promised to help me. I chided myself, "Oh Mamie, why are you even having these thoughts?" I needed to stop second guessing myself and resolved that it must be my inner demons creating this unhealthy doubt and mistrust of the people who loved me. I promised myself I would never again allow my mind to play tricks on me and to move forward without fear of being caught.

Of all things, I was given this disgusting homework assignment, right in the midst of my escape plans! I wondered if my teacher knew what was happening at home or was the topic of my assignment chosen by chance? I don't really believe in coincidence but you be the judge!

My assignment was to define what the words 'Mother' and 'Mom' meant to me and how they were different in meaning. How fitting that I would be grounded to do a homework assignment on this of all topics, on the very day that I would finally be released from my prison. Yes, this was my planned escape day! Remember, you're doing the judging...*fitting or coincidence?* I'll share my thoughts with you about how I struggled through it.

I referred to Sara as mother, not mom, which is more than my brother could bring himself to say out loud. Herb commonly addressed her as 'your mother' when he spoke with either J. Watson or I. He had no use for her and wouldn't dignify her by calling her by the respectable name of 'Mother'. Let's see if we can explain the difference in my mind and Webster's dictionary so you'll understand how I wished to refer to her in my homework for English class. Would you like to know how 'Mother' is defined? How about 'Mom'? 'Mother' meant *teacher, friend, provider, comforter, listener, and caregiver,* and not a single one matched how I felt about mine. Moving on to 'Mom' I discovered that the word was defined much the same as 'Mother' but expressed differently... *to take care of, loving, clothes cleaner, encourager and does what is good for a child!*

Oh my gosh, this was going to be difficult. My mother was none of those good things except perhaps the *clothes cleaner.* But wait, it was Colena who did the laundry according to mother's specifications, of course. After all, her children were to appear immaculate at all times as a reflection of her excellent parenting skills. And yes, I wanted my 'Mother' to be my 'Mommie' but the sad truth of it was that I resented calling her by either name because she didn't deserve that kind of respect. Would I be able to write what these words meant in my life? Would mother read them after I was gone? And so I ask you again. Was it coincidence that such a homework assignment, *intended only for me by the way*, was given on the very day of my escape with Daniel?

Here are a few more thoughts that crossed my mind as I struggled to complete my assignment. I would never dare to call her by her given name unless I was looking for some serious trouble. Maybe I should just forget about my plans to leave and stay home in the hope that my mother would eventually learn how to become a real 'Mom'. By now you can understand just how badly my reality was clouding my vision and why I found this assignment to be so conflicting. I reminded myself that I was deeply in love with Daniel and that I must follow through with my plans to be with him. Perhaps the words 'love' and 'survival' meant the same thing to me at that time.

Now it was time to put everything else aside and move forward with an entirely new life. Neither Daniel nor I had any clue about what would lie ahead. We only knew that we were finally on our way. He picked me up in grand style in a pink 1960 Lincoln Continental convertible no less. And wasn't I his 'queen for a day' when he opened the car door for me and allowed me to slide into the front soft leather seat to be by his side!

I pinched myself to see if this was really happening or if I was stuck in another of my 'wishful thinking' daydreams that had become a way of life for me. Playing on the radio was the song that we chose to be our own 'forever' song, *So Much in Love by the Tymes*. I settled back and relaxed, because I believed with all my heart that nothing could possibly go wrong ever again. And, why wouldn't I feel that way? We were in love and on the road to the rest of our loves together.

**Our first stop was to be at my grandmother's home.** I wasn't especially close with my Aunt Rosie, *as she preferred to be called,* but I did love her and believed that she would help us. She had nothing but contempt for her own daughter because of the way she had treated Herb for all of his young life so surely she would be the first one to understand why I so desperately needed her help. I knew that I wasn't her favorite granddaughter but I was about to learn a lesson about family loyalty which I would never understand to this day.

As Daniel and I approached my grandparent's large brick estate, we first noticed their luxurious white Cadillac with the classic fins in the driveway, telling us that they were at home. We planned to switch vehicles for a few days should anything go wrong. My parents would be none the wiser.

Daniel and I ran from the car to the rear entrance of the house, excited that everything was working out perfectly as scripted…or so I thought. Oh my God! Nothing could have prepared me for the shock that greeted us when that door opened. My grandmother had been expecting us and gave us the high sign to get out of there and to go quickly. I'll never forget her words. "We can't help you! Leave immediately!" I was stricken by the fear in her voice as she tried to help us in her own way. Her words left no doubt that mother had gotten to her with a made up story, designed to suit her own purpose. I could just picture her, snickering over a glass of wine as she savored the brilliance of her nasty scheme.

My grandmother gave me a quick account of what had happened. Mother had told them and anyone else who was listening, including my brother Herb, that Daniel was taking me to Florida to become part of a prostitution ring. Of course, we denied it vehemently. Surely they knew by now that my mother would stop at nothing to hurt me. I tried to make her understand that Daniel and I were in love and that we needed their help to escape the life of torture their daughter had inflicted upon me. But it was too late, mother's deceitful trap had been set and a whole new chain of events were set in motion.

It was time to run for our lives, our only chance to escape the fury of a mother scorned, as she certainly would be when she found out that we were making a run for it.

For the record, I do believe that my grandmother didn't believe the lie but being 'old school' she didn't quite understand the romantic way of doing things. She had been betrothed to her husband and that was just the way things were done in her world.

13

The Big Chase

Daniel and I had to leave now! We peeled out of my grandparent's driveway like a house on fire, not once looking back. Knowing my mother, she would have the entire Houston Police Dept. on our trail within minutes. We tried desperately to weave our way in and out of back streets in an effort to hide our highly noticeable pink convertible. Mother was like a bloodhound in heat and I had not become any wiser about escaping her wiles.

High hopes had filled our hearts when we started out that day. Now to be let down by my own grandmother came as a shock to both of us, definitely putting a crimp in our plans. Well, let me tell you, I wasn't about to give up now. Daniel and I were in love and we truly felt that all of our troubles were a thing of the past. A little crimp wasn't about to stop us. My spirits were still high and we would beat my mother at her own game. As we pulled into a parking lot for a reassuring hug, *I Will Follow Him by Peggy March* came on the car radio and I took it as a sign that we would always be together, that our plan would never fail as others had in the past.

I was still so young, barely sixteen yet had already been through more hell than most people suffered in an entire lifetime. Hope was all I had left with nothing else to lose so we were going for it and that was that. Every little while, I would begin to feel anxious and Daniel knew exactly what to do. He'd pull off onto the shoulder and cuddle me until I stopped shaking. This renewed my faith that anything was possible when I was with him. We would never turn back if we had anything to say about it.

After driving around for a while without being detected, it seemed that we may have been given a decent head start and didn't want to waste a minute of it. Perhaps this was the only assistance my grandmother could give us. We would never know. Readying ourselves for the next move, we turned in the direction of the railway station, believing that the airport would be the first place they would look for us. When we were within walking distance, we parked the car off the main drag on a side street and covered the rest of the way on foot. We rushed to get inside where Daniel bought my one way ticket to join his parents in Florida. As we headed toward the platform entrance, we could see my train approaching and I could literally taste the freedom that was mere minutes away. I stopped to give Daniel a quick hug that would have to last until we could rendezvous in Florida to be with his parents.

Without any warning, a strong sense of foreboding overtook me. Oh no, not again! I knew this feeling all too well. Daniel must have sensed my panic and as we turned to look, there was my mother and two police officers racing toward us. Daniel grabbed my hand and we ran for the nearest exit, not knowing where it would lead but fortunately for us, we were able to hide out in a small janitorial room until they passed by. We waited a few minutes before we exited and headed back to the car to collect our thoughts and plan our next move.

It made good sense to remain in the same area where they had already looked. We had spotted a small movie theater close by and decided to wait there until we felt safe to leave. Who would have guessed that the movie we saw would reflect our situation to a tee. It was about a young couple trying to escape a horrible past and begin a new life together. They too, were being chased by a relentless evil that eventually caught up to them. Their story did not end well, leaving me to drown in my tears. Sensing that this was a bad omen, I sought comfort on Daniel's shoulder, who reassured me that we would still make it to all of our tomorrows together.

When it seemed safe to leave the theatre, we headed for the bus station. As we rounded the corner, we noticed a few police cars at the entrance. We took off in the opposite direction and after about an hour of circling the area, headed back to try again. The police cruisers were gone and there was no sign of mother. This time, we not only parked a safe distance and walked back to the bus depot, but we disguised our appearance so as not to be immediately noticeable.

Anxious to make it this time, Daniel quickly purchased my ticket to Florida and after a quick hug, I boarded the bus. I kept repeating to myself, "Please dear God, keep us safe from my mother! Please give me a break for once!" While waiting for the bus to depart, an announcement came on the loud speaker, explaining that we needed to depart the bus and switch to another. I was panicked, knowing that it had to be her again…*who else would it be!* I quickly rejoined Daniel on the platform. He had just seen mother across the depot talking to the police. He grabbed my hand and we outran them again. Not knowing what to do next, we chose to drive around for a while and think about it.

The sense of doom was so pervasive I could barely breathe. It was becoming quite clear that we didn't have many options left. Daniel's parents had warned us not to cross the state line together, especially since he was over 18 and I was still a minor. Mother would have loved that and you can be sure she had that base covered. He'd be locked up and I'd be dragged back home again. What were we to do? Perhaps by now, mother would have exhausted her search of all public travel options out of the city, making it the safest bet that she would focus her efforts on the state line option. So we took our chances with the airport. What choice did we have? If God was truly on our side, mother would have been there and gone by now.

I prayed harder than I had ever prayed before. "Oh my dear precious God, I know that you love me. If you have anything good planned for me in this life, please let it happen now." I was still young and naive enough to believe that bad things should not happen to good people and that my time would surely come. I kept thinking those positive thoughts all the way to the airport. The stress of the day was taking its toll on both of us yet we refused to give up. We had been barraged with roadblocks every step of the way and we weren't about to stop now.

We stopped at a small chapel at the airport to pray for protection as though God might hear us better if we were in his house. Daniel had checked flight times and we had just enough time to catch the next plane out. If we missed it, the next one wouldn't be for another hour and we didn't dare risk waiting that long. We purchased my ticket and proceeded toward the gate, hoping that nothing would go wrong this time and that I'd soon be in the air. My heart was in my mouth the whole time, especially feeling the tension that Daniel was experiencing. He wanted so badly for this to go without a hitch and dreaded the possibility of my being sent back home and the danger that would inevitably await me there.

We were greeted by security guards when we approached the gate. My heart lurched as I could literally feel my life passing before my eyes. My knees were shaking so badly, I had to grab Daniel's arm to steady myself. Before they even stated their purpose, I was begging them to let me go. Daniel explained that I was being followed, that my mother was a serious child abuser and I was running for my life. It took a lot of persuasion but they believed him once they noticed my mother and Herb running down the aisle toward us. Rather than take a chance, one guard quickly escorted us to a private office out of sight while the other intervened with mother and Herb in an attempt to delay them. I showed the guard some of the heavy scars that I was carrying on my body and I could tell that he wanted to help. Thankfully, the guard kept us hidden until a new flight had been arranged in another area of the airport. I can't tell you how thankful we were for their help.

As it turned out, the security guards had clear reason to stop my mother and Herb after she told them that Herb was packing a gun and would stop Daniel at all costs. Of course it was a lie and she was scapegoating Herb as she always did with no regard whatsoever for the damage she was causing him. While they were detaining her, they escorted us to our new gate and assisted me with boarding. I started to breathe easier but experience had taught me to never feel safe so long as mother and I shared the same planet.

I was praying to myself non-stop, "Dear Lord, let this plane start moving now!" Instead of answering my prayer, the Lord presented me with a new twist of fate.

"Oh my God" I prayed. "Please dear Lord, let my eyes be seeing anything else but what's in front of me!" I was praying so frantically, I thought my head would explode. I could see Daniel from the window of the airplane. The two police officers with Herb and mother detained him. I was frozen on the spot hoping for the plane doors to close so that we could take off. And they did. We began to taxi when I reminded myself that it was okay to breathe again. I didn't want to leave Daniel in trouble but in my heart, I knew he'd be okay and would not have wanted me to get off that plane under any circumstances.

Just then, the plane came to an abrupt halt. Why are we stopping? I looked out the window and couldn't see a thing. But yes, we had come to a complete stop on the tarmac! Seconds later, I could hear the microphone crackle as the attendant made an announcement. "Ladies and gentlemen, we are making a brief stop but will take off again shortly. Please keep your seat belts fastened." I was drowning in my dread when the aircraft door opened and two police officers boarded the plane. They moved along the aisle, examining every face until they came to my seat. One of them asked if my name was

Mamie. I struggled to appear calm as I answered, "No, I don't know anyone by that name." Then he produced a photo and firmly stated, "Look missy, this is you and you need to come with us." I completely fell apart, thinking that I would collapse to the floor if they asked me to move out of that seat. In tears, I begged them to leave me alone. "Please let me get away from my mother. She's insane and she's going to kill me." My pleas had fallen on deaf ears. One officer wasted no time in pulling me to my feet. He grabbed me by the wrist so forcefully that I thought my bones were being crushed. Then we de-boarded and walked across the tarmac in the blazing sunshine. It was late in the afternoon and easily a hundred degrees outside. I was silently hoping that I would pass out and wake up in a safe place with Daniel by my side. I would not be so lucky. I was batting a hundred when it came to failure so why would this time be any different.

I had never come this far before and it occurred to me that I was about to face the worst night of my life. As I passed by Daniel, our eyes met and I'll never forget the tears of sadness that were streaming down his face, as he shouted out, "I love you Mamie. Don't give up hope! We'll be together soon." He had tried so hard to save me from mother's terror that he had put his own freedom at risk because he was of age and I was not. I never loved him so much as I did at that moment and so wanted to assure him that he had not let me down. Mother just didn't know it yet, but our time would surely come. Then Daniel disappeared because our special security guard gave him the high sign to take off because things were about to get worse for him.

Oh yes, you can be sure that I was taken back to 'her' house. It would be some time before I could bring myself to call her 'mother' again, but for the sake of this book, I must. It was no longer my house, but a prison that may as well have had bars on all of the windows, locking me up inside. My jailer knew nothing about being a mother and my dad was 'missing in action' as usual.

Once Herb learned of her deceit, he was totally livid. He was not a boy anymore and definitely had lost all fear of her when it came to his own welfare. It hurt him the most because she could still play him with her deception to the point where he had aided and abetted her to hurt me worse than she had ever done before.

Mother's appetite for inflicting pain never abated. It was typical of her to build strong connections both at work and in her social circles. I won't even speculate how she gained her power over people, but she was always able to call in a favor when she needed one. In fact, she used her connections to have Daniel fired from his job. He'd been in training as a journeyman for a promising position that meant a bright future for him. It seems that she used her story of trafficking in prostitution to get her dirty deed done. Had they not done her bidding, she would have spread that rumor throughout the industry, which would have hurt the business. It wasn't enough to use the knife on him but she seemed to get perverted pleasure out of twisting it as well. She had formed strong alliances with upper management and no amount of effort could get this firing undone. Daniel managed to extract the promise that as long as he never spoke of what had happened, they would never reveal the fact that he had been fired to any potential employer. They would simply explain that he had been 'let go' due to a slowdown in business.

Poor Daniel never was able to get work in the Houston area again. Was it because the story had leaked out or had mother herself, blackballed him in the industry. After all, no employer would want to take a chance having her anywhere near to their operation. She was a horror story and her reputation preceded her throughout the industry.

So now that mother had succeeded in ruining both of our lives, Daniel gave up his job search and joined the Army to pursue a new career as a military officer.

He applied to Officer's Training School in Georgia. What we learned later was heartwarming. Apparently Daniel's former boss still held Daniel in high esteem and without mother's knowledge, had given him a wonderful recommendation to help him gain admittance to the school. We had finally scored our first point against her!

After what Daniel and I had been through, things would never be the same again. I now had a taste of what it might be like to break free and felt certain that our time would come eventually. I hung onto that hope like a crucifix that mother could never take away from me. Had I given up, I don't believe that I'd still be alive today.

Yes, hope had kept me alive but dreaming was not coming easily anymore. What was the point! Dreaming was a punishable offence in my prison. I resolved to do my best to cope until I was able to legally walk out and never look back. Until then, I took her blows to my face, my body and my heart but she couldn't destroy my hope. I only knew that time would pass and my day would surely come.

Until then, I would find ways to contact Daniel at Fort Benning where he would be stationed for the next two years. On one occasion, mother caught me in a telephone booth. She just knew in her heart and mind that I was talking to him. "Excuse me, did I say heart and mind... *like she had either?*" Her first move was to rip the phone out of my hand. But there was something different about her this time. She was too quiet. Then she moved in close to me and pressed her lips against my ear without uttering a word for several seconds. And then she whispered the most hideous message into my ear. "Mama loves you baby. Come home with me now and I'll show you how much!" Her words chilled me to the bone and I just knew that I was about to graduate to a whole new level of terror. Then she took me by the hand and led the way home.

Once she had dismissed my Father and J. Watson, I could hear the slide of the dead bolt on the front door. Quite unexpectedly, I felt the strangest sense of peace wash over me and I understood that this must be my time. If it was her plan to kill me, I was okay with that. I would be free of her at last and she would certainly have to pay for her crimes. Had that feeling only lasted, I would not have had to endure what was coming at me next.

This time, her weapon of choice was a whip that she had bought in Mexico. Every lash tore into my body until even my scars were opened and spurting blood onto the wall behind me. She didn't stop until I finally crumpled onto the floor unable to move. I must have passed out because the next thing I knew, there was a basin of soapy water and a sponge beside me but mother was not in sight. The message I took from this was that I'd better get that wall cleaned up or phase two of my punishment would begin. I was too messed up to think yet I do remember vowing that she would never ever break my spirit! I would be with my Daniel one way or the other.

The next day at school, Daniel's friend Darren handed me a note in the hallway. I read and re-read that note to be sure that I understood it correctly. It read that Daniel had sent him a one way train ticket to his base town in Georgia, instructing him to give it to me in strict secrecy. I was to go straight to the train station immediately after school that day and he would meet me at the other end. Daniel would have my airline ticket to Florida and he would join me there on his next day off.

Mother worked late that night and I was well on my way before she had any clue that I was gone. And so I left with only the clothes on my back and the knowledge that I would make it this time.

Point two had been scored!

14

Making It on My Own!

1959 Hillman Convertible-Like My first Car

It had taken a colossal effort to get this far and I couldn't have done it by myself. All thanks to Daniel, I was ready to begin my new life and prove to myself that I could survive without my family. It seemed that I'd been pursuing this chance for most of my life and now, here I was. Although I struggled to keep positive thoughts in my mind, I had no way of knowing what challenges lie ahead of me. That great unknown would soon reveal its secrets and make or break me, but rest assured, I would give it my best shot. After all, failure was not an option for me. I had to make it on my own.

After I reached Fort Benning, where I reunited with Daniel, I began to feel safe again. Soon, I was enroute to Del Ray Beach, Florida where I finally met his parents who would provide food and lodging for me until I had a place of my own. Thanks to Daniel, his parents believed in me and it was easy to see where he got his kind and loving nature. I wished my parents had been like that. If they were, I would never have wanted to leave home.

When I arrived, Daniel's mother showed me to my room and lovingly suggested that I might want to freshen up before joining them for dinner. Everything in that room represented the warmth and security that I had longed for all of my life. The décor was all white and yellow and the sun shone brightly through a large shuttered window into a room that had never known sorrow. On the bed were towels with beautifully scented soap which I would later learn was eucalyptus and orange. "Even now, I can close my eyes and conjure up that enchanting scent and now that I think about it, I just might run out and look for some." I saved the best part for last! Along the wall at the end of the bed was a glass cabinet with multiple shelves from ceiling to floor. I bet you can guess what was in it! If you said dolls, you'd be right! At least a hundred dolls graced those shelves, as though they had been waiting for me to discover them. I had prayed for dolls from the time I was a little girl and in his wondrous way, God had given me dolls in abundance. I sent a little prayer of thanks for that special reminder that my prayers do get answered but in his time, not mine.

Once I was settled in, Daniel's mother took me shopping for a few clothes that I would need for my new start in life. After all, I had left home with only the clothes on my back and no money. When he left me at the airport, Daniel had pressed an envelope into my hand and told me that it contained enough money to see me through until I could get established.

With my new clothes, trendy haircut and fresh makeup, I boldly set out in search of work. After all, I didn't want to take their hospitality for granted, even if I did want to stay there forever to soak up the love. In no time, I found a night job with the telephone company, taking incoming calls on a switchboard. There, I would quickly learn a skill that would stand me in good stead for my future. To make ends meet, I took a second job as a desk clerk at an ocean side resort. I was working sixteen hours a day, but being so young, I felt that I could handle it until I was fully on my own.

Things came together quickly after that and I would soon have my own place. Daniel's family helped me to find a small duplex to rent and I bought my first car, a 1959 Hillman convertible. Now that was some car! It was all I could afford and it did look cute on the lot with the top down. It wasn't until I had it home that I discovered a gaping hole where a rear vinyl window was supposed to be when the top was up. Ever the planner, I figured that I would sew some plastic over that hole to keep the rain out. I could hardly believe that I was able to accomplish so much with one month's salary but it would not have been possible without the support of Daniel and his family.

At first, my new life looked promising but it wasn't long before my expenses exceeded my income. I had not factored the cost of food and gasoline into my budget and I was losing weight rapidly and becoming malnourished. When I first moved in, I found two small cans of food on the shelf. One was a small can of deviled ham and the other was chili peppers, if you can call that food. My first trip to the supermarket was disheartening but I knew that I had to be resourceful with the little bit of money that I had. I found a bag of tortilla chips and a package of cream cheese, figuring that the chips would stretch much farther than a loaf of bread.

When I got back to my duplex, a small basket of fruit was waiting for me outside my door. My landlord had left it for me as a welcoming gift. In it were three apples and two oranges but at least it was healthy food and when added to my meager purchases, I felt that I could get by until my next paycheck came in. Next, I mixed the devilled ham and chili peppers with the cream cheese, which made a very tasty dip for the tortilla chips, even if I do say so myself. Then I sat down and rationed out my food to ensure that it would last for the next couple of weeks. It worked out to five tortilla chips and a teaspoon of dip a day but it was the best I could afford until my finances improved. I figured as long as I had a roof over my head and any amount of food, I would survive, but for now, at least, a full bag of groceries was out of the question.

Oh my gosh, I couldn't believe that I was down to counting tortilla chips instead of sheep when my head hit the pillow at night but my dreams were all about cold Dungeness crab like Colena used to make for us with milk and cookies and fresh baked pie. I even dreamt of the times that I was sent to bed hungry as a small child and my midnight kitchen raids when mother and Colena were selling their delectable desserts.

I was determined to make it on my own and too proud to admit that I needed help. I knew in my heart that I only had to ask and Daniel's family would have been there for me. Perhaps I should have stayed there longer and saved my money for a while before taking on so much responsibility but they had already done so much for me and I refused to impose upon their kindness any more than I already had. Besides, they were away for a couple of months and I wouldn't be able to reach them anyway. I couldn't afford a telephone but Daniel would write and ask if I needed anything. I always assured him that I was doing just fine. I wondered if my healthy dose of pride was a sign of growing up or if it only served to drag one foot into the grave.

After a few months of this struggle, my day of reckoning finally came. No longer could I survive on five tortilla chips and a teaspoon of dip a day and five hours of sleep at night. Between car repairs and gasoline, I had nothing left over for real food at the end of the month and no relief in sight. My weight had dropped to eighty-five pounds and I barely had the energy to get out of bed in the morning. To make matters worse, Daniel had been shipped overseas and I had no idea when I would ever see him again. Pride had lost this battle and I was too sick to care anymore. So, with no money and no further need to remain in Florida, I bit the bullet and made plans to leave. I sent notes to Daniel and his family letting them know of my plans, explaining that there was no reason to stay there with Daniel gone and to thank them for being the family that I had so desperately needed.

As sick as I was, I had no intention of returning home to mother. In the shape I was in, I don't believe that my frail body would have survived another beating, much less my sanity. Fortunately, my last month's rent was prepaid, leaving me with barely enough to make the trip back to Houston. I called my aunt, *my mother's sister*, and asked if I could stay with her for about a month until I could get a job and find a place of my own. She was okay with that but something in her voice didn't sit right with me. I had learned all too well that when something sounded too good to be true, it usually was, especially in my family. I was really looking forward to seeing my two cousins again. Those boys were so sweet to me and loved me like the sister they'd never had. Now, at least I had a plan and so I readied myself to make the trip.

After I said my goodbyes, I packed the car and hit the road. I can't tell you how nervous I was about driving this cross country trip on my own. I was not an experienced driver and other than cross country jaunts I had taken with my parents, I had never driven more than a few miles on my own. When I was no more than fifteen minutes into my trip, I realized I had no idea how to get onto the Florida turnpike. I drove around for what seemed like a couple of hours until I was finally on my way, heading north. My plan was to clock as many miles as quickly as I could that day so as to reach my destination without too much delay.

Remember I told you that my rear vinyl window was missing? Well, that old expression 'don't put off until tomorrow what you can do today' came into play in spades that day. Seems I was always waiting for that spare bit of cash to buy the plastic and it never came. As luck would have it, at least my luck anyway, the sky opened up and that little opening sucked in buckets of rain like a giant sponge. I couldn't get pulled over quickly enough to get my clothes off of the back seat before they were drenched. Looking back, I can see the humor of that day. I was surely a calamity waiting to happen but at least I was trying.

Another fifty miles up the turnpike, my little dream buggy decided to give up the ghost and came to an abrupt stop right in the middle of the road. Thick black smoke was billowing out from under the hood and I had no idea what to do next. Now what? I searched frantically for my emergency flasher but couldn't find one. Perhaps my car was just too old to have that feature. It didn't take a master mechanic to see that I was in serious trouble here. At least I had the presence of mind to slip the car into neutral and push it over to the side of the road and that's where I sat, totally distressed and already exhausted. I would have given anything for some good healthy food but tried to put it out of my mind. Not knowing what else to do, I did what any normal sixteen year old girl would do—I cried like a baby and prayed a lot!

After about an hour, a woman stopped and asked if I needed help. I explained my predicament and that I was afraid to leave my car there. She agreed to hook up my car and tow me to the nearest exit. The fact that she even had the wherewithal to hook that car up convinced me that my guardian angel must have been watching over me. About five miles later we passed a road sign that read 'No Towing. If caught towing, drivers will be fined.'

Oh no, what if she had seen that sign and changed her mind about towing me off of the highway? Worse yet, what if we got caught? Well, that wonderful lady just kept driving and after about another fifty miles and several exits later, her blinkers started flashing as she prepared to exit the turnpike. I still had to deal with the cost of fixing the car. I only had about fifteen dollars to my name and that was earmarked for gas. I had planned on driving straight through to Texas and sleep on the side of the road when necessary because I had no extra money for food and lodging. I was hoping that my guardian angel would stay with me the rest of the way and help me to stretch my money until I made it back to Houston. My aunt made no bones about letting me know that I could stay with her but getting there was my problem. Cold, tired and hungry, I still had another eighteen hours to go.

After a while, I saw lights ahead which signaled that help might be near. Maybe now I'd be able to find a garage and get my car fixed that night and be on my way. Okay, watch me now, as I throw another of Mamie's plans onto the scrap heap of failed dreams! A huge lighted sign appeared at the end of the exit ramp: NO TOWING: VIOLATORS WILL BE FINED. As if that wasn't bad enough, the sign was on the property of the State Highway Patrol headquarters where a patrol car was sitting on the side of the road. Could it get any worse than that? What a dumb question that was. Of course it could. Didn't it always?

We had no choice but to drive right past them with my car in tow and wait for the inevitable sirens to start wailing. And wail they did and loudly enough to wake the dead. I can' tell you how badly I felt for that poor lady who was only trying to help another woman in trouble. I knew that I couldn't afford to pay any fines and was powerless to come to her rescue. I had to find a way to keep her out of trouble. I had no idea what her financial situation was or how I could possibly pay her back for being so helpful to me, but find a way I must. The trick was to find a way to get them to talk to me first. Before the officers could get to us, I leapt out of the car and flew into tears. "Officer, please don't blame this on her. She was only trying to help me get off the highway where my car broke down. She was afraid to leave me alone on the side of the road in a strange place!" My hysterics must have been convincing because that sweet officer took me by the hand in a gentle, fatherly way and instructed me to "calm down!" Still a blubbering and quivering mess, I flinched when he tried to hand me a hanky to dry my tears. Those officers must have realized that I was young and very much afraid.

After reviewing our ID and drivers licenses, they lead the way to a gas station that had a mechanic on duty. I had so wanted to hear good news about my car but the prognosis was anything but pretty. I needed a new radiator and the mechanic could not get one in until the next day. The work could be completed the following day and then I'd be on my way. Every cent I had to my name would only make a small dent into the cost of fixing that car and I had no idea how to make up the difference. If it was possible for my world to end that day, I'm quite sure that it would have.

For someone who was accustomed to panicking at the mere sight of a police officer, I have to admit it was refreshing to see the human side of these two. They suggested that we put up for the night in a nearby motel where I'd be able to dry my rain soaked clothes and get a good night's rest. Not wanting to admit my plight, I begged off the motel idea by explaining that we needed to make a few phone calls and would check in later. I wasn't comfortable with the idea of sharing a room with a stranger even if I could afford a room. On the other hand, vagrancy was a serious violation that wasn't so appealing either.

It turned out that my traveling companion was running away to escape her abusive boyfriend so we had more in common than I realized. In retrospect, I now believe that she was an answer to my prayers when she rescued me from the dangers of the Florida Turnpike. We were quite a pair, much like characters in a novel— *Peyton Place* comes to mind or a modern day *Thelma and Louise*. Okay, you guessed it, *Thelma* parked her car behind the gas station alongside mine, preparing to sleep for the night. I, *Louise* did the same except that my pillow was a pile of wet clothing. It seemed safe enough since the station had closed for the night when the officers left. Gosh, I was so tired that it didn't even occur to me that a gaping hole where a window was supposed to be might have invited dangers too scary to think about. But the last thing ether of us expected was a fairy tale ending. No more than an hour into an uneasy sleep, I was awakened by the bright light of a flashlight shining through my car window. I was petrified beyond belief.

It seemed to me that we just might have pushed our luck to the breaking point. It was our friendly police officers again and I was sure that we were in big trouble now—that would be us, classic vagrants sleeping in cars. Now they knew that we'd lied about going to a motel so it was time to spill the beans about our hopeless situation. We were cold and hungry and I, at least, didn't have the money to eat, much less pay for my car to be fixed.

Had anyone told me there was such a thing as angels in blue, I would never have believed them, given my history of the great blue pursuits my mother had instigated. Our heroes took us to a motel and paid for our rooms, one night for my friend and two nights for me while I was waiting for my car to be repaired. They even paid for my repair bill as I had no one to turn to for help. When I heard the magic words, "get showered and dressed and we'll be back in an hour to take you both to dinner," I honestly thought that I'd died and woke up in Heaven. "Yes God, I never really doubted you for a minute!"

My friend and I were only about ninety-nine percent certain that these guys were on the level, so we contrived a backup plan just in case their motives were less than pure. Yes, my friend was of age but I was still a minor, a serious issue for the officers if they were up to no good. When we arrived at the restaurant, it was closed. Just then, the door opened and one of our police friends beckoned for us to come inside. Oh my goodness, I was so caught off guard when we were greeted by a huge crowd of well-wishers who had no other motive than to take care of us and keep us safe. It seemed that every on and off duty police officer and their families were there to welcome us, feed us and give us money to get us to where we were going. The story of our plight had spread throughout the station and they had all decided to help. Other than Daniel and his family, I had never known such compassion. I think that I hugged everyone in that room at least twice and thanked them through many tears of gratitude. "Didn't I tell you that I had some good memories to share with you? It'd be pretty hard to top this one don't you think?"

Two days later, I was on my way again in my little jalopy which had mysteriously sprouted a new rear window. Even the 'gas fairy' had paid a little visit and gifted me with a full tank to see me the rest of the way home. My friend had left the day before to finish her trip.

The state patrol had gone one step further and telephoned my aunt to let her know what had happened and that I appeared to be ill. I was looking forward to a nice warm bed and getting back on my feet again but before I even arrived back in Houston, my aunt had changed her mind about allowing me to stay at her home. It was bad enough that she called my Mother in Las Vegas, where my family now lived, to come and get me, but she had the gall to concoct a dirty little story to make matters worse for me. I wasn't even there yet, but seemingly I was already a bad influence on my cousins and had tried to sleep with them. My Mother obviously took her word for it, no matter that I wasn't even back in Texas yet. Talk about two people being 'cut from the same cloth'—deceit was a family trait it seemed. It was one thing to have second thoughts about taking me in, but quite another to do it so ruthlessly.

When I arrived at my aunt's, my Mother was waiting there to drag me back to Las Vegas with her. She showed me no mercy, despite the fact that I was so terribly sick and underweight that I could barely stand. But what did I expect from a parent who had never given a damn about my welfare anyway!

Among other things, I swear my Mother was a magician. She could make anything disappear, especially a little convertible car. I suspect that she gave it to one of my cousins but not a penny showed up in my pocket. She said that my car was an embarrassment to her but more likely, it was because she didn't trust me to drive alone to Las Vegas.

15

My Senior Year

1965

The trip back to Las Vegas was uneventful. When we got back, I had no choice but to resign myself to a life of Hell until my eighteenth birthday when I would finally be able to walk out that door a free woman. "Yes, I said woman!" My time away had helped me to grow up. More importantly, I would never be making those same mistakes again. I couldn't quite make up my mind if it had been safer to be out on my own and starve or to be in prison with my mother and at least get to eat three square meals a day. Something inside of me had died. Life had betrayed me in the worst possible way and I just didn't have the strength or the will to fight it anymore. So here I was in Vegas, braving up for the next chapter in my life.

Before long, the 'thought police' were at work again, invading my every thought and penetrating my sleep at night. Apparently I was committing thought crimes and we all know that mother had no tolerance for that. In true form, she meted out what she felt were appropriate punishments but I was so numb with indifference, she wasn't getting the same pleasure out of hurting me as she usually did.

I returned to Bishop Gorman High School where I had enrolled when we first moved to Vegas after one of my parent's many splits. Mother warned me that the Priest and Nuns would keep a close watch over me and I wouldn't get away with ever running away again. Little did she know that I had always wanted to attend a Catholic school, not quite understanding why, but hoping that I'd be able to find some peace in my life if I did. Mother hated the Catholic faith but this was her way of keeping me in check and as far away as possible from those 'wild kids' that attended schools in the public system. She wanted me in a closely guarded environment where she could watch every move I made.

It took a while but my physical health gradually improved. Strangely enough, the distraction of my school work and new friends had a healing effect on my emotional wellbeing. I was learning to dream again yet still had no desire to make any new plans, or shall I call them schemes. Instead, I'd travel in my mind to places that soothed me in times of trouble and stress. For me that was the ocean's edge, the only place on earth where I could find true inner peace. Somehow, mother had managed to rip me away from my beloved beach and all she could offer me now, was a desert of burning sand. I contented myself with knowing that time would surely pass and my day would finally come.

Anyway, my senior year turned out to be quite different than anyone in the family had expected. Just as I had hoped, I was able to find a measure of peace in that school and in my extra-curricular activities. I joined the choir, learned Latin and found myself among friends who really and truly cared about one another. This was definitely not the prison atmosphere that mother expected it to be. The nuns were not mean old shrews who took joy in chastising us into shape with ear pulling and hand slapping with rulers; in fact, quite the opposite was true. They treated everyone in our class with the utmost respect and went out of their way to prepare us for life after graduation.

Our school had a chapel where we were allowed to enter at any time. This was especially helpful for me when I needed a private place to think and to be alone. Sometimes, after a particularly bad run in with my mother, I'd find myself there, trying to recover and find a way to deal with the emotional pain. It helped to light a candle for others who were in trouble and one for myself when I was feeling especially torn up inside. Mother didn't know about that and I wasn't about to tell her. I was just thankful that I finally had a place to go where I wasn't afraid and felt protected.

My mother still wanted to control every aspect of my life and wouldn't allow me to make any decisions that really mattered to me.

I suppose she didn't think that I had enough to do, despite piles of homework so she decided that I would take a job working for her sister, Elaine, at the motel that she owned and operated. You might say that she threw me to the wolves but I'm happy to report that it backfired quite nicely on her. As it turned out, I rather enjoyed working there and before long, had excelled at every aspect of my aunt's business. I quickly learned how to check in guests courteously and efficiently, work the switchboard, assist with bookkeeping, manage housekeeping personnel, and even performed higher level public relations work. When I was caught up with my work at the motel, Elaine would send me across the parking lot to a building she rented to a medical practice. My work there was to back up their office staff when they were getting behind. Between the jobs I held in Florida and now with Elaine, I was building a fairly decent list of skills and experience for my resume and a work ethic to be admired.

Aunt Elaine certainly lived up to her reputation for being a tough task-master. She was known for being deeply set in her ways, demanding and inflexible. You just knew that you had to do it her way or hit the highway, so to speak. In so many ways, she was like my mother. They both had such a low expectation of me that I was hell bent to prove them wrong. The fact that I cheerfully tackled every challenge set before me caused Elaine to reassess my value as a family member who could easily measure up against old country standards. I had found my element and it didn't hurt my self-esteem one little bit. I look back fondly on that time because for the first time, I had managed to impress someone in my mother's family.

When I became ill with a severe cold, Aunt Elaine became unusually concerned about me and came to the apartment to see how I was doing. She demanded that my mother pamper me to help break the fever and lung congestion. In fact, she made me the mother of all hot toddies and forced me to drink it down in a single go. Being my first alcohol drink ever, it really knocked me for a loop but she knew exactly what she was doing. I slept through the rest of that day and most of the night and was ready to tackle school and work the next day. For a girl who was never wanted, I do believe that she began to care deeply about me and called me her 'broken bird' which likely drove my mother mad!

All in all, life wasn't as bad as I expected it would be in Vegas. I was growing up and though I was still at loggerheads with my mother, she was preoccupied with her own social life most of the time. Las Vegas offered her the social opportunities that she craved so deeply.

When we first moved to Vegas, Aunt Elaine set us up in a very prestigious apartment building. Mother had yearned for such an address throughout her many years of marriage to my father and had spent all those years pretending to be a member of the country club set according to her upbringing. Now there would be no more pretending and I could only hope that her change of status would somehow have a positive effect on her parenting skills. Mother hosted fabulous parties at the apartment and invited the most renowned celebrities you could ever imagine. I met people like *Dick Shawn* from *It's a Mad Mad Mad Mad World, Robert Goulet, Harry James, Greta Garbo, Big Band singers* and if you can believe it, even *Danny Thomas.* "Oh my goodness, can you imagine how thrilled I was when both *Danny Thomas* and *Robert Goulet* kissed me on the cheek?"

I loved those parties for many reasons but I had to admit that it was good to see my mother shed her rigidity for a change and let loose. She was truly in her element and wasn't paying much attention to what I was doing for a change. I was enjoying my new found liberation and allowed to feel the music and dance the night away with the rest of the party. We even danced the Dabki and the Belly

Dance that my grandmother had taught me as a child. I was very good at it too and attracted a lot of attention from our guests. I can't begin to tell you how good it felt to be treated with respect for the first time in my life. Oh, what a whirlwind life we were leading.

Though mother had only painted negatives about my Aunt Elaine, I came to realize that she was the more loving of the two, despite her tough exterior. I was the only one who she trusted to do her most confidential work. Although she called me her "broken bird" because she knew my heart was broken, she often told me to never give up and to always remember that my spirit cannot be broken if I just hang on. Now, my aunt was by no means an angel. In fact, she had the reputation of being as cold, cruel and calculating as my mother, especially toward my older brother Herb. "Now isn't that interesting. Seems that both she and my mother could only manage to feel love toward one child." For my mother, it was J. Watson, and in time, Aunt Elaine came to love me. Fortunately, for Herb, he had our grandparents who loved him unconditionally.

Word had it in the community that Aunt Elaine was mafia connected but who knew for sure…certainly not anyone in the family that I knew of. Even mother claimed that Elaine had once put a hit out on her, but didn't say why. She did have a certain reputation as a business owner in Las Vegas and had no pity for people who had gambled away everything they owned and tried to run out on their motel bill. I myself heard her comment, "God help them if they don't pay my motel bill." I didn't want to know what that meant.

My aunt's affection for me was exactly the kind of protection that I needed. The only person that my mother was afraid of was Elaine and she feared the consequences if she stepped out of line with me. Yes, mother had lost this battle and I was one giant step closer to winning the war. All I had to do was hang on for another year so that I would finally be free.

My friends at school were so different than any I had known in Texas. We enjoyed debating issues, some not so nice and others challenging. They seemed to enjoy the Texas slant to the issues which added some spice to the mix. We were all fast friends and stood by one another whenever needed. One guy even borrowed my driver's license to get his underage girlfriend into the casino one evening. Sixteen was the admissible age and I was at least that. When he returned it, I was surprised to find that he had altered the birthdate to show that I was eighteen and had even laminated it to be more convincing. These were the ways of teenagers back then and I seemed to fit right in.

"I just learned that my 50th high school reunion is coming up and all being well, I will be there to reunite with my old friends." That was the only school year that mattered to me, a year in which I made good friends and was reasonably out of reach of mother's wrath. J. Watson and I grew a bit closer that year. Though he was one grade lower than I, we did share one class together which was taught by Father McCarthy, one of my favorite teachers ever. He prayed with me often, bolstering my hope in ways that I didn't even know existed. Because of him, I grew more closely attached to the Catholic faith. He seemed to understand that I was a lost soul who was struggling to find my place in the world. I believe that he entered my life at a time when he could do the most good toward healing my damaged spirit. It was Father McCarthy who encouraged me to get involved in school projects and extracurricular activities. Becoming an integral part of the school body agreed with me and reassured me that I was no different than other girls my age, despite my devastating past. He even understood that it was normal for young adults to waver between responsible and inappropriate behavior and knew exactly how to steer us back onto the right path. One case in point was my huge crush on the football coach. Rather than lecture me, he encouraged me to get involved with the school paper, poster design and other creative pursuits. I even signed up as assistant director for the senior class play production, all of which managed to buy me some distance from my mother and of course, that football coach who would have been all wrong for me anyway.

I poured my entire energy into this production and there were even times that I was trusted to direct it on my own. Ken, my senior director, was on loan from another school and we became fast friends in no time at all. I had great respect for his talent and he taught me well. Our cast mates had other ideas though. Some of them wanted to see a much closer relationship between us despite the fact that I wasn't interested in him in that way. Of course, I kept it strictly professional at all times. I was still teased about it and wasn't surprised to find many suggestive references in our yearbook.

Looking back, that last two years had been eventful when it came to boyfriends. I had lost Daniel, who had been shipped out by the Army to Vietnam. As much as I tried, no one would tell me how to contact him. And earlier this year I had met an alumni who had graduated that year and sadly, I lost touch with him too. He left to join the Navy and sailed off to join the war in Vietnam. Before leaving, he gave me his football jacket to remember him by. It seemed like everyone I had ever cared for was gone, thanks to that horrible war.

Thankfully, Aunt Elaine had more authority in my life than mother during my senior year. When a school trip to Disneyland and Sea World was organized for graduating students, it was Elaine who came through for me. I never did figure out what hold Elaine had over my mother but it did the trick where I was concerned. She believed that I had earned a break and so it was a done deal.

The trip would buy me a week away from home and I can't tell you how much I relaxed once those bus wheels hit the pavement. Of course the trip was chaperoned by nuns so we just knew that no monkey business would be allowed. Even mother was reassured that I couldn't get into any trouble with nuns on board. We had such a blast on that trip, even dancing on the bus to our favorite music...*I Can't Get No Satisfaction* by *The Rolling Stones, Woolly Bully* and many other wonderful selections from the 60's charts! These were happy times, so unlike my first unfortunate trip to Disneyland.

Toby, one of the most popular boys on the trip, came down with the measles on the very first night. He was relegated to his room and wasn't allowed to leave, having to take his meals in the presence of the nuns instead of his friends. What a downer that was for him and it didn't sit well with the rest of us either. So, we put our heads together to figure out a way to spring him so that he could enjoy his trip along with the rest of us. The year was 1965 and I can still visualize our typing teacher together with some other escorts, sitting around the pool with their eyes trained on our rooms to ensure that no one strayed and that Toby stayed put.

Where there's a will, there's a way as they say and I just happened to be the experienced planner in the group. Here's how it went down. Toby's room had a connecting door on both sides, a little fact that had been overlooked by our chaperones. One of the girls was about Toby's size so we borrowed one of her outfits. All I can say is he wore it well and once he had donned a hat and sunglasses, he passed perfectly as one of the girls. We escaped through that connecting door and actually passed by, incognito, right under the noses of our guards. Disney was the magical kingdom after all and it was time to party!

It wasn't long before we were missed but we had so much fun dodging our chaperones that it just made our day. We spent hours on the rides and in and out of the buildings before our luck ran out and we were cornered. I needn't tell you how angry they were that we had gotten away with it for as long as we did. We all figured that we'd already been exposed to his measles so why not let him enjoy the magic with us. We were teenagers for crying out loud! As luck would have it, several other kids did get sick but we had our good time and even the return trip was just as much fun. What we didn't count on were the angry parents who were there to greet us when returned home. Oh, you can bet that mother was among that group and just assumed that I had been the sole instigator. Although I'd hatched the plan, it had not been my idea to spring him in the first place. I was never sorry for helping my friends and nothing she could do would ruin this very special memory. There were just too few of them in my life.

I still had to face the music when I got home. Before we were even in the door, I was besieged with the crippling fear that at any moment, she would turn into the ugly monster I had learned to hate so intensely. I won't go into detail about what she did to me that day but I will tell you that I just couldn't take it anymore. I'd had a taste of freedom and I knew that I could never go back to the way things used to be. I needed to leave to save my sanity and I had to do it soon. I had been caught up in this sick cycle of abuse all of my life and had never given up hope that my mother would someday love me, until that day. I finally accepted the fact that it was never going to happen.

Sick with discouragement, I slipped back into my world of day dreams. I imagined what it would be like to be rescued by my prince charming and live happily ever after. I know that sounds naïve for a seventeen year old but at that point, I needed so badly to feel good again that I allowed my imagination to take over. Of course, my dream life was viewed through rose colored glasses and my prince would never hurt me under any circumstances. But that wasn't the way things were in the real world, at least not the world that I knew.

Nothing could have prepared me for what happened next. I knew that I had to leave and settled for the first opportunity that came along. I put myself in harm's way again but this time, I had no one to blame but myself. My prince charming actually did come along but not in the way that I had expected.

About four months away from graduation, I met a handsome young man who would soon make a huge impact on my life. We met on a blind date with friends and it didn't hurt that he drove a hot car, a Wildcat convertible to be exact. I felt an instant attraction to his charismatic ways and he sure did have a fascinating way with words. I was enchanted with this man and couldn't see the trap that I was about to walk into.

16

My Last Escape from Home

So just who was this special young man? Was he not the same man who I thought would save me once and for all? Stay tuned…more to come on that hot topic! I seemed to be second guessing myself at every turn yet my need to leave the torture behind far outweighed the nagging little doubts that plagued me. I simply put it down to my past track record coming back to haunt me.

I had hoped to wait until my eighteenth birthday but an opportunity to escape had presented itself and I planned to leave shortly after graduation. So imagine my surprise when my family picked up and moved to Redding, California before I could get away. That move came out of nowhere but I decided to make the most of it and go with them anyway. After all, I could as easily leave from California, couldn't I? Once we completed our move, I decided to fast-track my career path by enrolling in a nursing program at a community college in Redding. The idea of helping others who had endured abuse in their lives was already taking shape in the back of my mind and nursing seemed like a good place to start.

Every spare moment was needed for studying but it was nearly impossible to focus while my parents were fighting the next revolution right outside my bedroom door. Their battle lines were drawn and I could no longer cope with their screaming and slapping, day and night, non-stop. I finally resolved to get out of this hopeless excuse for a family once and for all. I only had a few weeks to go until I was legally of age and no longer saw any purpose in waiting. This time it would be for good although the saddest part was leaving J. Watson behind. I would miss him terribly but hoped that I could work something out with him down the road. So here I was, nervous about leaving but more afraid to stay. I knew that I would reunite with Herb once I was settled but didn't hold out much hope that I would ever see my mother and father again. That's how serious I was about never coming back! And so, on a beautiful sunny day in

August, 1965, I left with suitcase in hand to begin a new life, only glancing back once to say my final farewell.

I drove my car to a drug store parking lot in Redding, parked it and got into the beautiful chariot that awaited me! Yes, it was that very same light green Buick Wildcat convertible that I told you about before I left Vegas! My knight in shining armor was Barry, a charming, handsome devil if I ever saw one. Sure, I had nagging little twinges of doubt but was so anxious to move forward with my life, that I ignored them completely. It was easier to believe that he would love and take care of me in the way that I needed so badly. In time, I would just have to learn to love him back.

I was filled with anticipation as we headed east toward Las Vegas where Barry was living. As we approached, we could see the brilliant lights of the strip, lighting up the sky as if to welcome us home again. It was all so alluring and I couldn't wait to start our new life together. Our first stop was at a small wedding chapel where we tied the knot and spent our first night together as man and wife. The act of becoming a woman that night was everything that I'd hoped for and then some. I think that I completed the act of falling in love that night and I have to say, his sexy good looks didn't hurt a bit.

Laying low for the next few weeks was our top priority since we couldn't risk being seen by anyone we knew, especially my Aunt Elaine, who might feel obligated to 'spill the beans' to my mother. Once my long awaited eighteenth birthday came and went, we picked up the phone and together, called both of our parents and made our announcement. I can only tell you that it didn't go over well with any of them, especially mother.

You might say that we honeymooned in Vegas and then settled down in Redding. Barry had been working in a gypsum mine but had better plans for our life together. He didn't see much of a future in Vegas as he had no intention of working in a mine or the service industry for the rest of his life.

Eventually, he convinced me that we could build a better life in Redding, and at the same time, show my parents that we could make it on our own. Maybe then, they would finally come around and my nightmare would become a thing of the past. I wasn't even sure that I wanted to see them again, much less win their approval but I agreed with Barry that it was high time that they learned to respect me for who I was and for the mature direction I was heading in. I confess that I had no such expectations but I wanted to please my husband and so we made the move back to Redding.

In no time at all, we found the perfect home and set up housekeeping. The house was brand new and was the envy of our friends. For all intents and purposes, I looked like I finally had it made. Barry was an excellent provider and I really didn't want for anything except that all was not as well in paradise as I had hoped for. I was discovering that Mother was the devil I knew and Barry was the devil I was just getting to know and I couldn't tell who was the worse of the two. I had jumped into a relationship that threatened to be even more dangerous than the one I had escaped from. His problem was excessive drinking and if I'd seen this in him before we were married, I would have run as fast as I could in the opposite direction.

Barry did what every bad drunk does when under the influence of alcohol. He beat on me unmercifully without a trace of love in his soul. In that dreaded state, he had no recall whatsoever, that he had just loved me tenderly mere hours before. This was a man who drank till he dropped because just one more was never enough. I soon learned that his Jekyll and Hyde behavior would vacillate between tenderness and extreme violence, even worse than I had grown up with. At least mother didn't need a drink to release her demons but I suppose you might say that a tall, husky man had more physical strength to destroy his prey.

If you think that my self-esteem took a beating, you'd be right! In my mad rush to escape my living hell at home, I had actually 'jumped from the frying pan into the fire'...*just a little more cliché if you don't mind!* This was not what I had bargained for. I had made my own bed and now I had to find a way out of it. Yes, there were short stretches when all seemed right but invariably, his next spree would be more terrifying than the last.

One of those times when all seemed right in my world turned out to be the worst nightmare of my life. "My friends, I can't even begin to recall every lurid detail of that night but I promise that I'll share what my heart has allowed me to remember."

It all began on a beautiful summer evening. The clouds were the purest blue that I'd ever seen and all felt peaceful and calm in my world. My fickle heart yearned for this to be the sign of better times ahead but like a fool, I didn't know that it was too good to be true. We decided to barbecue that night and while I prepared the food in the kitchen, Barry headed to town to pick up some snacks. When he returned, his arms were loaded up with beer...*enough to entertain an army.* He wasted no time putting down the first few beers while I sat frozen, dreading the inevitable personality change that was taking shape before my eyes. And just like clockwork, the horror began!

Barry forced me into the house with a loaded gun held to my head. I knew that the gun didn't have a safety and feared that it would go off at any moment. He threw me to the floor and spit in my face, warning me, "You are mine and you'll do as I say, when I say!" Then he raped me over and over again as though he didn't know when to stop and couldn't even if he wanted to. He was as out of control as I'd ever seen him. When he was done, he rolled over to catch his breath. I hoped that he would pass out so that I could get out of that house and run for safety. I managed to stand up and stumble out the door, then ran like a mad woman through the woods along the Williamette River and hid behind the brush and the trees. I kept looking back over my shoulder to see if he was on my trail. When he caught up to me, he held me by the neck and dragged me back to the house. My screams of terror must have rung out loudly through the night air but no one came!

Later that night, when Barry was in the shower, I hurried to the phone and dialed 911, begging them to hurry because he was threatening to kill me. The police arrived and quickly assessed my physical state and then I had him arrested. Believing that I was safe for the rest of that night, I rushed around, throwing some clothes and necessities into my suitcase and put out some calls to make arrangements for somewhere safe to stay for a couple of days. My friend Pauline urged me to come to her place, and assured me that I'd be able to stay as long as I needed to. I agreed to be there early the next morning before Barry was released. I had every good reason to believe that I could get out but another bomb was about to drop on me.

About four in the morning, mother got a call from Barry from the jail. He urged her to come quickly and bail him out. He explained, "Your daughter had me arrested for no reason at all and we need to get to her before she can leave me." Without giving it a second thought, mother raced to the jail house to bail him out. Within two hours, he was on the doorstep screaming at me to let him in. Fearing for my life, I raced toward the back door and through the back yards to my doctor's house down the street. Their son, Rusty rushed to let me in while his sister Catherine ran upstairs to wake her parents, shouting, "There's a crazy man in the driveway and a lady is yelling for help!" Dr. Mac and his wife Martha ran to the upstairs window. Barry was in the driveway and it wasn't a pretty scene. He was in a blind rage, and threatening my life, while waving a knife in one hand with his pistol in the other. "Get out here you little bitch! I'll kill you if you don't get out here right now! I'm gonna teach you a lesson you'll never forget!" My heart sank when I saw my mother standing right behind him, lending encouragement and moral support to him, instead of helping me, her daughter who needed her now, more than ever. I'll never forget what she was yelling out to me. "Mamie, get out here now and face up to your husband. You made your bed, now lie in it!" Then she was gone in a flash. I suspect that she didn't want to hang around for the neighbors to see, lest it damage her social status in the community. She was such a hypocrite!

After a while, things calmed down outside and it appeared that Barry had given up and gone home. I felt terrible about Mac's kids having to witness such a terrible scene and made the decision to go home and if I was lucky, Barry would not be there, or at worst, he would be passed out, sleeping it off. Mac walked over with me and together we checked out the house and Barry was nowhere to be found. He left and I locked the doors. Then I raced around to grab my bags to load the car so that I could leave right away for Pauline's house. I almost made it. Just as I was leaving, Barry exploded through the front door with such force that it knocked me to the floor. Then he kicked me in the head and reopened the wounds from his earlier assault. I was screaming hysterically as he dragged me down the hall toward the kitchen, petrified at what he was planning to do next.

The next thing I knew, the police were there and slamming the cuffs on Barry for the second time that night. My screams had awakened my neighbors and someone had called 911 to come to my rescue. An ambulance arrived to administer first aid and determine the extent of my injuries. By this time, my eyes were swollen shut and I was covered in my own blood. Fortunately, I didn't require any stitches and all I could think about was getting as far away from that house as I could. The young police officer reminded me that the only way they could hold him was if I pressed charges. I agreed and they shoved him out the door and into the cruiser.

After they left, I ran to the bathroom to clean myself up, praying non-stop for God to keep me safe until I could get to Pauline's house. Within minutes, I was in the car, without daring to look back.

My friends, "I can't tell you how traumatic it's been to relive the events of that dreadful night. After days of tears and a major anxiety attack, I've managed to get this much down on paper but for now, I need to distance myself from it for a few days before I can tell you the rest of the story." I had buried those memories and bringing them to light after all these years was the same as living them all over again.

Barry was locked up for the night and I was beginning to breathe easier now that I had settled into my room at Pauline's house. I desperately needed a hot shower to wash the blood from my hair and to survey the damage done to my face. In the meantime, Pauline scooped up my clothing and threw them into the washer. Feeling refreshed and clean again, I slipped into my nightgown and joined Pauline in the kitchen over a hot cup of cocoa.

I managed to get a couple of hours sleep before Pauline woke up her baby girl for her morning feeding. The comforting aroma of bacon and eggs lured me into the kitchen and I was beginning to feel human again as I sat down to eat. Before I could get that first bite off of my fork, I was overtaken by an unfamiliar queasy feeling in the pit of my stomach. I wasn't surprised after what I'd been through since the night before. My little dog, Gidget was snuggled up to my feet and I felt a sense of normalcy returning to my life.

I was in the kitchen washing up the breakfast dishes when I heard the doorbell ring. Pauline went to answer it and lo and behold, there was my mother, pushing her way into the living room, calling out my name. You guessed it, Barry was right behind her. She had actually bailed him out for the second time in a few hours! In that moment, I was so far beyond panicked that I started to hyperventilate. Through it all, I could hear the hateful words that she spewed in my face. "Now what have you done to provoke your husband? You've always had a way to make everyone hate you and you end up getting exactly what you deserve."

Barry had finally sobered up and didn't grasp the seriousness of what had happened between us. He begged me to come home with him and promised that it would never happen again. "Baby please, I need you to come home and we'll start all over. I promise that I won't hurt you again. Please come home with me now." I couldn't go with him and in my heart, I knew that I would never go back to either of them. I told him that I needed a couple of days to heal and then we'd see if our marriage could be rescued. That seemed to placate him and they left. Around ten in the morning, Pauline had to leave for work and drop the baby off at the sitter on her way. She told me to get some rest, to keep the door locked and stay close to the phone.

When she was gone, I finally broke down and cried like a baby. Every dream I ever had was shattered and I felt disconnected from my life as I had known it. I was pacing back and forth and little Gidget was shadowing every step I took, as though she was telling me that she loved me and would protect me no matter what. My mother's final words kept echoing in my ears and I couldn't shake them off. Maybe she was right. Maybe I was a loser and impossible to love. "Mommy, why did you do this to me? Why couldn't you just love me like you do J. Watson?" I needed so badly to have her hold me for the first time in my life and to make me feel safe. A deep sense of hopelessness and despair filled my entire being and I knew that I had reached the end and couldn't do this anymore.

I searched the medicine cabinet and found a bottle of Pauline's tranquilizers. They were outdated but I figured they'd do the trick. I downed them all, hoping by the time anyone found me, it would be too late. Then I laid down on the floor with Gidget, hugged and kissed her goodbye and sobbed myself to sleep. My last thoughts were of Herb and J. Watson, hoping they would forgive me for leaving without saying goodbye.

From what I was told later, Gidget had run to the window and started barking frantically as she scratched on the window pane to get the attention of anyone nearby. The next door neighbors rushed over to see what was wrong but when I didn't answer the door, they phoned Pauline at work to let her know that something seemed to be wrong. Pauline rushed home to find me on the floor. I vaguely remember her shaking me and begging me to come around. "Damn it Mamie, wake up! You can't let Sara win! Please don't die on me my friend." An ambulance arrived in minutes and rushed me to the emergency ward where a tube was placed down my throat to pump the pills out of my stomach. When I started to come around, I had the sinking feeling that I had failed again. I couldn't even do this right. Why had they bothered to save my miserable life? I kept repeating the words, "Please let me go...just let me go."

I had no health insurance so I was transferred to a county hospital. When I woke up, I discovered that I was in a padded lock-up...a psych ward to be exact. Now what was I to do with that?" I'd gone from one prison to another and couldn't find any way out! Claustrophobia was gripping me by the throat as I screamed for the nurse to let me out. "Oh dear God, let me out of here!" The duty nurse came in to settle me down with a shot of something in my hip. She reassured me that the doctor would talk to me tomorrow and until then, they had to keep me in this room to keep me from hurting myself. It was standard treatment for a patient who had tried to take her own life. The medication worked and I did calm down but it would be some time before I would ever open up again. The doctors tried for weeks to get me to talk but I couldn't see any point and I had stopped caring anymore. When I was finally able to express my feelings again, I had an outburst in the doctor's office that said it all. "If you let me out, I'll tell you how many ways my mother hates me and how many beatings I took and how many scars I carry in my heart and on my body! Now let me out!" There it was! That one brief statement said it all. My secret was out and it took the fear along with it. I had never told anyone about this terrible secret between my mother and I and strangely enough, I felt surprisingly relieved for having it out in the open.

My doctor informed me that this was only the beginning of my treatment but I was now on the road to recovery. He did sign me out after another couple of days, but only after I promised to stay in treatment. When I walked down that long hallway and through those locked doors, I knew that I would never look back. My most pressing worry was that Barry knew exactly where I was because my big mouth mother felt more obligated to tell him where I was than she did to protect me.

I went back to Pauline's house after being released from the hospital. My mother paid me a visit that day to deliver a few choice words but before she could open her mouth, I jumped all over her. "You've hurt me for the last time mother. Whatever you have to say to me, just spit it out, then leave and don't ever come back." I had caught her off guard but that didn't stop her. According to her, I was a disgrace to the family and she'd no longer give me the time of day. "Why didn't you behave like normal girls do instead of shaming me in front of my friends?" None of this came as a surprise to me. I'd heard it all before and I was finally building up a protective shell to keep her out. She wanted to know what I did to provoke Barry to mess up my face so badly, claiming that I always did have a way of making people hate me and deserved everything I got. Then she hit me with the lowest blow yet. "Don't think that you'll ever see Herb again! He's washed his hands of you and never wants to see you again!" If anything could break my heart, it would be losing Herb and she knew it.

I knew that I had to deal with Barry sooner or later so after a couple of days, I met him at the house to talk over what was going to happen next between us. He was back to his usual charming self and acknowledged that what he did was wrong. He begged me to forgive him and give him another chance. Had I not been down that road before? Of course I had but once a fool, always a fool, as they say. After all I'd been through, I still opened my arms and forgave him. Resisting him was the furthest thing from my mind for the next few hours until I finally fell asleep in his arms. When I awoke, he was gone. He had left for parts unknown and had only wanted his way with me one more time to end it on his own terms.

He returned a couple of weeks later and I told him that I wanted a divorce. His eyes turned as cold and black as I'd ever seen them and I knew that meant trouble. He was sober but the look in his eyes gave me shivers up and down my spine. It turned out that he had been checking up on me through my mother who told him to get home right away because I was pregnant with his child. He stood before me in silence when suddenly he raised his hand and reached into his jacket. Just as I expected him to shoot me on the spot, he pulled out a bottle of whisky, uncapped it and started to guzzle it down. I'd never seen anything like it before. He emptied that bottle and smashed it against the door, sending shards of glass in every direction. Then he grabbed me by the neck and spat out the words, "So we're pregnant are we! We'll just see about that!"

Before I could run, he was on top of me and I thought he was going to rape me again. Instead, he ripped off my clothes and tried to reach inside of me to kill our child. He was kicking me so hard in the stomach that I threw up from the pain. Then he turned away and walked out the door. After that, I never saw him again. I miscarried that night and because of the trauma and damage that I sustained, I was never able to conceive a child again.

Cruelty knew no boundaries when it came to my mother. Christmas had come and I was yearning to see my father and my brothers again. I had to see for myself that Herb still loved me as he always had and so I went home for the holiday. I'd been feeling so lonely and I just needed so badly to feel his strong, protective arms around me, making me feel safe again. Gift opening was fun until mother presented me with hers. Every package I opened contained baby clothes. I didn't know that my heart could break in so many ways but when she noticed my tears of sadness, all she could say was, "Well, I didn't want to unwrap them!" This time when I left, I just kept walking.

17

On My Own, Again

Kecia

So here I was, newly divorced and eager to turn over a new leaf and get on with my life. I prayed that I would make better life decisions this time around, but then, I had no idea what a normal life even looked like. I must admit that I was nervous starting out. I was caught somewhere between being a child without love and an adult desperately seeking it, not realizing that this was a shaky foundation to build a new life upon. Because of my past, I was still struggling emotionally and I surely didn't know where to go for help. "This was the sixties and that vast social support network that we know today, barely existed back then."

There was one big positive in my life that I did find reassuring. I had survived a lifetime of the worst kind of deprivation and abuse that life could possibly deal out, yet here I was, stronger than ever and finally free. At least that was how I was thinking at the time. I fantasized non-stop about becoming a responsible adult and some-day, to be the best mother a child could ever ask for. I made a com-mitment to myself to live my life joyfully—no more struggling but a whole new me. Yes, I was the master of my own destiny now and was determined to embrace a life of new and exciting possibilities but I had no idea where to begin. "But then, I ask you, did that ever stop me?"

And so I moved forward, blinders and all, in search of that one great love story which would allow me to live happily ever after. I really did try, but I still drifted in and out of relationships, each one more toxic than the last. "Guess what! I never saw them coming. After all of my bad experiences, I had not learned a single thing about how to pick the men in my life?" Everything I knew about love would fit into a thimble and I continued to look for it in all the wrong places. It seemed that I lacked the instinct to choose any kind of friendship wisely and as always, I ignored every little warn-ing signal that nudged me to walk away.

"My dear readers, allow me to share a sad event that really did open my eyes." I was still living in Redding and trying to put my life back together. I met a young girl who I'll call Nina. She was anxious to make a new friend to lean on for moral support. I felt tremendous empathy with this girl and quickly became her confidante and as it turned out, her 'go to' person when she found herself in trouble and in need of help. Nina was a very sweet girl and before long, she confided in me that she was in an abusive relationship with her boyfriend, Tim. Oh yes, I could surely relate to that and knowing first hand that it never gets better, I pressured her to dump the loser. Tim was into drugs and when he was high he'd beat her so badly that she should have been hospitalized but he would never allow her to seek any kind of medical help. It broke my heart to see her this way but she lacked the courage to leave. She wasn't the fighter that I had become and made no effort to get away from this creep. I hated him for what he was doing to her.

I had a job at an answering service and was looking for a second job to increase my income enough to get by. Nina recommended me to a guy she knew on the police force who might be able to get me into a decent paying job at the station. I met Jack and we became fast friends in no time. He was most understanding about the abusive life that I was trying to leave behind. He took me to a police picnic and introduced me to some of his buddies on the force and he further helped me out by introducing me to his boss. This led to a volunteer assignment that I loved and I couldn't have been happier.

In the meantime, I moved in with Nina to save money so that I could pay off the debts that Barry had run out on. The worst of that picture was that most of those debts pre-dated our marriage. I had tried to reason with his debtors but for the most part, they were unforgiving and relentless in their collection attempts. Eventually, I was served with papers to garnishee my wages. I flew into tears when the Sheriff served me, right at the office no less! I was indignant and didn't try to hide it. "You can't get blood out of a turnip, can you?" I suppose he found that amusing because he replied. "Yes honey, but you are no turnip and may God help you!" "Looking back, my remark was rather comical."

I didn't want to lose my job but department regulations didn't allow employees to have any serious financial issues. In no time, I had worked my way up to the medical board and radio dispatch and was well liked and respected by everyone at work. In fact, I was even nicknamed *Gravel Gertie* of *Dick Tracey* comic fame. I had been sick with the flu and laryngitis and it was my doctor who had dubbed me with that name. It got around work and it stuck. Oh, it felt so good to finally belong somewhere and being treated as an equal and I didn't want it to end. I did manage to keep my job but at least that garnishee taught me a lesson. "So let's see now—a roof over my head or pay my ex-husband's debts! It didn't take a brain surgeon to figure that one out." I immediately filed for bankruptcy, hoping to put an end to this mess once and for all.

Coming home from work always made me nervous. More often than not, Nina and Tim had been fighting and had done their usual making up routine with alcohol and drugs. They'd be so spaced out that it was impossible to carry a lucid conversation with either of them. Nina was completely under his control and it was pointless to try to help her because he'd only retaliate by abusing her more. I even threatened to report him to the police but that low-life just laughed in my face. I should have seen the writing on the wall because he really didn't take kindly to threats. I wanted very badly to move but I was still out the money that I had loaned to Nina for the deposit on the house and it was impossible to advance another one for a new place.

The truth is that I had always been outspoken and often forgot to weigh the consequences before opening my mouth. I reminded myself that I wasn't a child anymore and no one was going to backhand me for speaking my mind so I didn't expect what happened next. Tim got even in a way that I couldn't possibly have expected. He laced my meatloaf with enough marijuana to send me into *never-never land* for a couple of days. Tim and Nina kept me outside in such a deep stupor that I couldn't move, even to go to the bathroom. It didn't help that they kept forcing pot laced sandwiches into me, keeping me in that helpless state with no chance to surface. When I did finally come around, I was furious. I had lost all respect for my so-called friend and her loser boyfriend. If Nina wanted to be his punching bag, that was her problem. It was not who I was or ever wanted to be. Dreaming was my escape from reality but never drugs! "He needed to pay!"

That had happened on a weekend and I had a court appearance to hear my bankruptcy case on the following Monday. I was still in a subdued state but I did manage to get through that hearing with a ruling in my favor. Yes, I faced legal restrictions for several years but that was so much better than living with Barry's debts or any reminders about him for that matter. I could now file him away into the trash pile that was my past and never look back.

Jack was livid when I told him what Nina and Tim had done to me, and understood that I needed to get even. He asked me if I wanted him to set up a sting to take Tim down. Naturally I agreed because that guy needed some serious payback. Well, I was about to learn another lesson! The sting was set up to take place after dark one evening. The police task force set up their observation point at the back of the property, hidden by an orchard that surrounded a pond in a park like setting. The plan had them hiding out there until I gave them the signal that a drug negotiation was in progress. I was shaking in my boots as I waited for just the right cue when money was ready to be exchanged. At the crucial moment, we were all interrupted by a loud splashing sound coming from the back yard. A police officer had fallen into the pond as he was moving into position to make the raid. I was horrified! These drug dealers were carrying a lot of money and with guns drawn, were ready for what happened next.

I panicked as I flew to the door, screaming at the officers to get in there and then I ran for cover. I didn't see what happened next but the sting did go down and the guilty were carted away in a paddy wagon. That was a close call for me and there wasn't any doubt that Tim and those other dealers knew that I was responsible for the takedown. Looking back, I should have moved out and just left it alone. Now I'd have to look over my shoulder for as long as I lived in that town. Jack sent a couple of his friends to move Nina and I out and to relocate us to a safe place where it would be hard to find us. For my own safety, I had to quit my volunteer sting operations with the police department.

I could only think that a lifetime of abuse had damaged my ability to reason. "How could I have possibly believed that getting even was worth risking my life?" I'd been blinded by this need and hadn't given a second thought to the potential consequences. That's what I meant when I said that I suffered from a condition known as poor judgment!

After all these years, I finally understand just who I was getting even with that night. Oh yes, I truly was the master of my own fate except that I didn't master it very well it would seem. Low self-esteem played a very large role in my ill-fated decisions and I blamed it all on my mother.

Our little hideaway was located on the outskirts of town in a very nice district, overlooking a beautiful lake. I spent many hours on that shore, contemplating my future and calming my fears. Occasionally, I ran into people I had known when I first moved to town. If you can believe it, one of my former friends told me that she had run into Daniel. Apparently when he recovered from the injuries that he'd suffered in Vietnam, he spent his entire leave on a quest to locate me again. He had traced me to Redding but never did find me before he had to leave. Had I known that he was in town, I'd have moved Heaven and earth to be with him again but I suppose that it just wasn't meant to be.

In a manner of speaking, I was standing on my own two feet. Maybe I shouldn't have been so hard on myself but those were hard times for me, especially when it came to my finances. In order to get by, I needed two jobs and thanks to my recent getaway, I was on the job market again, seeking to boost my income. I continued to work at the answering service where I got a tip about a job as a waitress in the restaurant at a local bowling alley. I had no clue how to do it but was always eager to learn and that was good enough for them. And so I chalked up another credential for my resume.

Now that job was certainly an eye opener for me. I knew that customers come in all shapes and sizes but no one warned me about the practical jokers. I served in the bar on my first night and wouldn't you know it, my first customer just happened to be one of those! He ordered a steak, and as I was trained to do, I asked him how he wanted it cooked. "Titty pink," he replied and I was horrified! "How was I to tell the chef how to cook this steak?" True to my nature, I rose to the challenge and headed straight to the counter to place the order. The chef became impatient as I stammered around trying to get the words out. "Hurry up girl! I don't have all day." When he saw my tears, he headed for the bar in time to catch my customer taking bets with his buddies on how I'd handle it. He came back with a big grin. "It's okay honey, I know. I'll tell you how to handle that character."

When the order was ready, I took it to his table wearing my prettiest smile ever. "Here's your steak sir—titty pink, just as you like it." It wasn't hard to figure out who lost that bet. The guy dug into his pocket and pulled out a twenty dollar bill and pressed in into my palm. "Here honey, you earned this!" Twenty dollars was a huge tip back in the sixties and I'd earned it on my very first order. Yes, I'd proven once again that no one could break my spirit.

My boss was so impressed that I didn't run for cover from those tough guys, he offered me a job as a cocktail waitress in the bowling alley. Apparently, he didn't realize that I wasn't twenty-one yet but since this was where the best money could be made, my age remained my secret. This was a big turning point for me. I loved that job and the tips were amazing. I served twenty-one lanes and handled it so well that I was offered Saturday nights as well because it was their busiest league schedule of the week.

I worked hard and saved as much money as I could so that eventually, I'd be able to drop my other job. After a while, I was beginning to wear down and I knew from past experience, that my health would suffer if I kept up that pace for too long. Sure enough, I developed what I thought was a bad cold but I kept on working. I didn't know it yet, but I had pneumonia and it wasn't going to get better on its own.

It was on a Saturday night when I finally got my wake up call. I had grown so ill that I could barely walk and yet I still insisted on making it into work that night. It was customary for two employees to handle the Saturday night business but the other girl didn't show up for work to help me out. All twenty-one lanes were filled that night and I was running off my feet trying to keep up with their cocktail orders. My favorite league was a group of doctors that I'd been serving from the beginning. They were so much fun to serve and it didn't hurt that their tips were right up there at the top. On this night, Dr. Gonzales observed that I wasn't feeling well and reached up to feel my forehead. I flinched when he touched me but he assured me that he wasn't trying to hurt me but was concerned that I didn't look well. I was burning up with a fever but I begged him not to say anything because I needed my job.

All I wanted to do was get this shift over with and go home to sleep. When I got outside, that nice doctor and his peers were waiting for me and offered to drive me home. I trusted them. They were doctors after all! Gratefully, I accepted their offer but collapsed before I even made it to the car. The next thing I knew, I woke up in the intensive care unit in an oxygen tent. I had double pneumonia and those nice doctors had saved my life. Sadly, my true age became known after this hospital incident and I lost my job serving cocktails. They kept me on in the restaurant but there wasn't enough money there to get by and so I moved on.

So there I was, forced to start all over again. I never seemed to have any trouble finding new work and before long, I was settling into a new job, one that would introduce me to my best friend in life, Ganelle Swanson. This was a friendship that would last a lifetime and as you can see, I dedicated this book to her memory. "I'll tell you more about Ganelle later in my chapter called Sweet Memories."

The years came and went and life was more or less the same...in and out of relationships and essentially, just getting by. In some ways, I was too trusting but all too often, my past would come back to haunt me in ways that would set me back emotionally for weeks at a time. "In retrospect, I should have sought out professional help and learn how to release my demons once and for all but instead, I just shut them out and buried them six feet under." After a lifetime of abuse and failed relationships, I came to understand that love wasn't going to find me in all the wrong places and so, always the dreamer, I set my sights much higher. I would find my prince charming and settle down to make babies. I wanted so badly to be a mother and to love and be loved in return and so I charged headlong into my next big mistake. "To this day, I ask for God's forgiveness because this was one mistake that not only hurt me, but the lives of innocent children as well."

That's when I met Andrew, a widower with two beautiful little boys. Could it possibly be any better than that? These darling little guys needed a mother and my heart felt so ready to be their dream come true. Our relationship blossomed and we knew that we wanted to spend our lives together. We married and I adopted the children as my own. Life was good and love would finally conquer all, or so it seemed. It took a lot of time and patience to compensate for the loss of their mother. I, of all people, understood how it felt to mourn the loss of a mother's love, even if it was under different circumstances. I tried to make it up to them but for reasons that I couldn't quite understand at first, I was ill equipped to show them the love that they needed. That's when it finally dawned on me that I had never learned how to give love, only to need it. No thanks to my mother, the cycle was now complete.

I wanted so badly to make things work and to give those kids the love that I'd never had. Right or wrong, I decided to invite my parents back into my life in the hope that they would find it in their hearts to be loving grandparents. Time would tell if this was a mistake.

Andrew knew my story and tried to compensate for my shortcomings as a mother. He knew how badly I longed to love a child with all of my heart and so we planned from the beginning to try to adopt a baby girl. I dreamt of spoiling her in every way possible to make up for the deprivation I had suffered as a child. So for months I wrote letters to every adoption agency in the USA and abroad. Then, right out of the blue, a TV program called 'Sins of Fathers of Vietnam' came on and after watching it, I knew that I had to follow up to see if a baby was available for adoption. We were thoroughly vetted as potential parents by child agencies who conducted endless home studies and interviews but it was well worth it in the end. I even had to write a report about my own life, our families and how I planned to enrich the life of an adopted child. That was the most challenging part but I must have done a reasonable job because we were approved and put onto a holding list.

And then the waiting began. We suffered through many letdowns and setbacks but the first good news came after two years. We were to become the parents of a baby daughter from Vietnam. Andrew and I were ecstatic and set about decorating the nursery …pink, of course! "I can't begin to tell you how anxious I was while waiting for her arrival. I longed to hold her in my arms and love her forever." The agency called to let us know when our little one was placed on the plane and gave us the arrival time and instructions to follow at the airport. And then in a heartbeat, our dreams were shattered. We were watching the news and they reported a plane from Vietnam had crashed and killed most of the passengers on board. Oh no, it couldn't be. Not after all this time. Our baby's room was ready – all pink with a crib, rocking chair and every baby toy you could possibly imagine. And then the dreaded call came, telling us that our sweet daughter had perished in the crash.

Our tragic loss was devastating. To add to the pain, we had to figure out how to tell the boys what had happened. They had shared in every detail of planning her arrival, right down to choosing her name. They were so excited about having a new baby sister in the family. The next day, the agency called back and asked if we would take an older child. They had a little five year old girl but she was sick and couldn't travel until she was healed. Of course we wanted her and set about exchanging the baby furniture for a little girl's. My heart was broken about our baby girl but if this child needed a family, we wanted to be there for her.

I would not rest until that child was safe in my arms and we could truly call her our own but it wasn't to be. Tragedy reared its ugly head again and ripped another child out of my arms. Her health had taken a bad turn and she passed away. I was hysterical and angry that this could happen twice, not only to us but to these dear little children whose only need was to have a family to love them. I wanted to talk to God about it but what was the point. The damage was done and I could only hope that those babies were in a better place. A few days later, Andrew returned our little girl's furniture because I couldn't bring myself to enter that room. My expectation of a happy ending was no more and I was sinking into a deep despair.

A week went by and another call came in from the adoption agency. She only asked one question. "Are you still hoping for an infant?" My first reaction was that I could be in for another letdown but without hesitation, I screamed out, "Of course I am!" Had my prayers finally been answered? I was instructed to be at the airport in three hours to pick up our new baby daughter. I didn't even ask how old she was. I just scrambled to get that nursery set up again, picturing her sweet little face on her fresh baby pink linens, with her very first teddy bear propped up in the corner of her crib.

I was overcome with excitement and had to share the good news with everyone I knew. Then I headed to the airport to pick up my new little bundle of joy. Andrew met me there and we waited, anxious to raise that identification sign when they arrived. The agent had described the woman who would be carrying our baby and when our eyes met, I think I forgot to breathe! She was really here and I couldn't begin to describe the joy I felt when she was placed into my waiting arms. She was sick and malnourished with a big tummy and a rash on her tiny face but to me, she was the most beautiful baby in the world. As I held her close for the first time, I whispered in her ear. "You will never want for love or ever be abused again. I love you already my little one." As we were preparing to leave the airport, my Mother made her grand entrance, wanting to see her new granddaughter. As usual, she didn't have anything nice to say but I was secretly hoping that she was prepared to be a real grandmother to our baby.

On the following day, my very special friends came to visit. No, not my imaginary ones though they would have been welcomed with open arms. It was Ganelle and her partner Pete and it was love at first sight. My heart was bursting with pride and joy and we chose this special occasion to ask Ganelle to be Godmother to Kecia… *the name we had chosen for our daughter.* Ganelle was so unlike my mother who had been cold and reserved when she first saw Kecia at the airport. I did have concerns about that because mother had always had a preference for boys. I was completely oblivious to the fact that I was doing the same thing to my sons, except in my case, I was clearly showing a preference for girls. I wanted so much to give her every drop of love I never had that I ignored the fact, these little boys also needed a mother's love.

After a few years of marriage, Andrew and I bought the five acres of land that was situated next to my parents. We built a beautiful home that most would only dream of and set up a hobby farm on the extra acreage. The kids loved the cows and the pigs and happily worked alongside of us as we tended to the huge garden that we'd planted. Life seemed to be going our way and all of the kids finally lived close to their grandparents.

It wasn't long before mother was driving a wedge between Andrew and I by showing a clear preference for our boys and ignoring Kecia. This was history repeating itself and sure enough, my resentment toward the boys became a serious issue between my husband and I. "Why couldn't I see what was happening? I was ignoring my sons just as my mother had done with me. It broke my heart but I was unable to stop myself."

The damage was done. Andrew was no help at all. He was hyper critical of everything the kids and I did. Those boys needed both of their parents but sadly, they weren't getting the love and support that they deserved. I tried so hard but I just didn't know how to give it to them. What a vicious nightmare our marriage had become. Andrew withdrew completely from Kecia and looking back, I'm not even sure that he had ever bonded with her in the first place. Neither my parents or Andrew showed any affection for my little girl. I became fiercely protective of Kecia and finally, the ties that had bound us together as a family finally broke.

It seemed like there was nothing worth saving in this marriage. I'd suffered many forms of abuse in my life but with Andrew, it was different. He was an emotional abuser and that was just as painful as a physical beating could ever be. He would give me the silent treatment for months on end and all it took was the slightest issue to provoke it. It could be as simple as finding a bit of dust on a shelf or in a corner and it would set him off. He was so obsessed with cleanliness, the first thing he did when he got home from work was put on a pair of white gloves and survey the house for evidence against me. If he found it, he stopped communicating with me for ridiculous periods of time, leaving me with only the children to talk to. I'd been willing to put up with it as long as he was a good father but even that changed. He became cold and nasty with the kids and that's where I drew the line. I would protect Kecia at all costs but I had no control over how he treated his own children. I know he loved them but increasingly, he lost his ability to show it.

I packed up our things and Kecia and I moved out, leaving Andrew and the boys behind. I missed them terribly but I couldn't remain in that loveless home a minute longer. It takes two to make a marriage and two to break it and I'll always regret the part that I played in hurting them because I couldn't control the demons from my past.

At least with Kecia, I knew how to love unconditionally and was completely fulfilled with the love that she gave in return. I gave everything to her that my Mother had never given to me and it spelled L.O.V.E. She has long since forgiven everyone who caused her pain. Heck, she even forgave me for smothering her with my excessive doting.

In many ways, history had repeated itself but I vowed that I would do whatever it took to break that cycle.

18

My Own Family

Kecia, Doug and Mamie

Sorrow was my constant companion, reminding me every day that I had lost the family that I hoped would last a lifetime. It was a marriage that couldn't be rescued but I will always regret the part that I played in failing those two little boys. My first responsibility was to make the best possible life for myself and my daughter, Kecia.

Like shades of yesterday, I found myself working two jobs to get by. One of my jobs allowed me to keep Kecia with me when she was not in school. I was doing mobile insurance exams which required that I visit applicants in their homes or at their business, to take medical histories. Most of the time, I was able to take Kecia inside with me but there were times that I had to leave her in the car for twenty minutes or so when I was meeting with a client. I hated to leave her alone like that and ensured that she had every possible distraction to make the time pass quickly. Not many children got to watch TV in the back seat of the car in those days. Between that and books to read or color, snacks and a blanket and pillow to rest her sweet little head on, she was one contented little girl. With the car door locked, I felt that she was safe and warm and only seconds from my reach.

 My second job was performing EEG's at an office while she was in school. My boss was also Kecia's Godfather and he had no trouble with her being there when I had to work outside of school hours. Those times were rare and usually only when I was on call at the hospital late at night and had to take her with me. I like to think that those experiences strengthened Kecia and helped to shape her into the responsible young woman that she is today. Her strong work ethic and deep love for her family are values that make me the proudest mother who ever lived.

"Now, fast forward to February 1986 when I first met Douglas Earl Adkins." While I didn't want to push my luck, I confess that I experienced a strong sense of déjà vu when I first laid eyes on him, as though I already knew that he would be my soul mate forever. It was Easter Day when we first started dating but a deep connection was already forming and it promised to last a lifetime. This may sound contradictory but time seemed to stand still when we were together yet always managed to pass so quickly. Doug was a man who had never been married and at the age of thirty-four, he still had a genuine innocence that was pure and refreshing.

Being on my own with Kecia had taught me to love unselfishly and to put her welfare before my own. I was a good mother to Kecia and if a situation or relationship was not good for her, then I quickly moved on. I had no such worries about Doug. He was a natural, giving father type right out of the gate and I trusted him with our lives. Never before had I known such happiness and I reminded myself every day to nurture it and not sabotage it in any way. "As you read this, please forgive me for gushing but Doug was all of this and so much more." I wanted to spend my life with him but wondered if he shared the same intent.

By the fall of 1987, I finally got to meet Doug's younger brother, Russell. He and his wife, Donna, came to meet us and we hit it off right away. It was Sadie Hawkins weekend and the five of us spent a relaxing day roaming around the Seattle Center. I had a sense of family peace that I'd never experienced before and I knew that life was meant to be this way. Throughout that day, Donna shared many warm family memories and my love for Doug grew even more if that was possible. I knew beyond all doubt, that he was the man I wanted to spend the rest of my life with.

Later in the day, Donna managed to get me alone for a few minutes to give me some advice and this is how it went. "Mamie, now that I'm getting to know you, I can see that you're the best thing that's ever happened to Doug." And it got even better, when she added, "Since its Sadie Hawkins Day, why don't you take advantage of the opportunity and ask him to marry you? I know he'll never make the first move on his own." This was a wonderful way to tell me that I would be welcome in her family and so I decided to take her advice. Donna and Russell left shortly after dinner and I knew that I only had a few hours left to do the deed. I rehearsed it over and over in my mind until I felt ready to put myself on the line. Finally, with only fifteen minutes left, I knelt in front of him and blurted it out. "I love you Doug. Will you marry me?"

"Oh dear, I was so not ready for his reply!" He thought about it for what seemed forever before he gave me this surprising answer. "Well, I need to think about it!" I was so shocked and embarrassed that I had put myself out there and this is what I got in return! My reply was sharp and quick. "Never mind, I take it back!" Now Doug is a highly empathetic man and I think he knew how upset I was. True to his word, he did think about it and a few days later, he came back to me with his reply. I'll never forget those beautiful blue eyes when he asked me, "Do you want to get hitched?" For such a romantic man, getting 'hitched' was not how I expected him to propose to me. I had dreamed about roses and champagne and maybe even a skyscraper message with the words 'I love you Mamie' trailing across the sky for all to see! But my man was not the predictable type and so I cried out to him, "Oh yes Doug, I'll be proud to be your wife for the rest of my life!" There, the deed was done and I knew that I'd be with my heart's desire till the very end.

Our wedding plans moved along quickly and we set the date for August 6th, 1988. We called his parents and then told my family.

As might be expected, my parents had no intention of attending and seemingly, overlooked the courtesy of sending their best wishes. This was Doug's first marriage and I had never been married in a church, so imagine how excited I was to enter into counseling to be married in the Catholic Church! I chose Kecia to be my Bridesmaid and Ganelle for my Matron of Honor and I was never as proud as when J. Watson agreed to give me away.

When our big day finally arrived, I couldn't believe how sweet and handsome J. Watson looked when he arrived at the church with his beautiful family. We had long before mended our fences and he was stepping up for me with nothing but the greatest love in his heart. As he walked me down the aisle, I actually felt a little giddy as we approached the man of my dreams. All my eyes could see was that hand-

some man, standing proudly next to my beautiful daughter by the altar. What more could I ask for but the love of both brothers, my sweet daughter and my soon to be husband! Yes, this was the single most perfect day in my life.

Life was good! We spent our honeymoon on the coast. We both loved the peace and serenity of the ocean's majesty but for the first time, I didn't need to go there to feel safe. Then we headed back to pick up Kecia to travel for a few weeks to visit our families in

Montana, Colorado and Wyoming. "What a whirlwind time it was for all three of us!" We were quickly adjusting to our new lifestyle as a family and simply adored his relatives. My goodness, they were almost as sweet as he was so it was easy to see why he was so easygoing and endearing.

Business had prevented Herb and his wife Diane from attending our wedding so it was a special treat for us to spend some time with them in Jackson, their home town. They loved seeing Kecia again and together we enjoyed a fabulous day taking in the sites and activities in the local area and then we ended our visit with a grand dinner out on the town. Our time with them can only be described as glorious.

Doug's family embraced us and honestly, that was the first time in my life I had known a family that wasn't dysfunctional. Doug's two sisters, Aline and Gail, both worked in the medical field—two of the most compassionate and caring people I'd ever met. You already met his brother Russell but there were two others, David and Brian. But here was the best part! Doug's mother was everything, and I do mean everything, that my own mother wasn't. We bonded immediately and Kecia finally had the grandparents that she deserved. "I think I hit on a valid truth when I met Doug's mother. Most of the time, you really can 'judge a book by its cover' and that particularly held true when it came to Doug and his mom.

Shortly after we settled down to married life, I began to experience some health issues. I was feeling sick most of the time and it turned out to be my diabetes. I had spent many years in denial about it, mostly because, as a single parent, I could never afford to buy the supplies I needed to keep it under control. It wasn't until our vacation in Hawaii that we both realized how bad it was becoming. Doug set about learning everything he could about this dreadful disease and made it his solemn mission to get me back on track—no more denial and to follow my doctor's instructions to a tee. He took care of me and I thanked God every day for bringing him into my life.

"Hallelujah! I would have shouted it from the rooftops if I hadn't been afraid of heights!" For the first time, all of the puzzle pieces fit together and oh, that picture was grand. Kecia adored her new Father, who quickly adopted her to make her his own.

Moving ahead several years, Kecia had developed into a beautiful young woman. She had overcome all of the difficulties from her early childhood, adjusted well to a new family and her self-confidence blossomed because she knew that her parents loved and supported her no matter what. She joined color guard in high school and shone her special light in many extra-curricular activities. Doug and I were very active in her school programs and accompanied every performance in and out of the state for her color guard activities. We volunteered everywhere possible so that we could always be close to our amazing daughter and sometimes that meant chaperoning on school bus trips. I'm immediately reminded of a trip that took us from Bremerton, Washington, down the west coast to San Francisco, California. Oh what fun we had on that trip with a full bus load of excited teenage girls.

As a family, we traveled to Hawaii, Montana, Colorado, California, Wyoming and so many other beautiful locations. One year, we spent our Christmas vacation in Whistler, British Columbia where Kecia polished her skiing skills. "By now, you know how I love to plan and our trip to Whistler was right up there as one of my best! I'll share more of that later in 'Sweet Memories'.

 Before Kecia graduated from High School, Doug and I opened a candy store. We made a fabulous selection of candies and truffles right on the premises and it wasn't long before we were a huge success. Our work schedule was staggering but we loved the business and put our collective heart and soul into making it work. Doug was already working full time at the local shipyard but still joined me at the shop every day after work. Getting to work side by side with my husband was the highlight of the entire venture for me.

The beginning of the end came when we employed my parents at the store. It was a foolish move and I should have known that it could only end in disaster. In the beginning, mother seemed to respect our decisions and surprisingly enough, was easy to get along with but it didn't last. The 'old mother' showed up one day and never left. She was moody and bossy and when she didn't get the last word, she simply refused to do her share of the work. If I wasn't picking up her slack, I was putting up with her criticism. Even when I had surgery on both feet, she refused to carry her weight. It didn't matter to her that I was not supposed to be on my feet until my stitches were removed. All I got from her was, "Stop being lazy and learn to stand on your own two feet!" Good old dad just sat idly by and, as usual, refused to step up.

In the meantime, Kecia was accepted into Washington State University on scholarship. Doug and I were beside ourselves with pride. Our sweet little girl was finally all grown up and ready to make her mark in life. That being said, my heart was breaking at the prospect of being separated from her for long periods of time. By the time we travelled to Eastern Washington to deliver Kecia to her new residence, I was a complete basket case. For me, it was the saddest trip of my life and I wondered if other parents felt the same way. "Of course they did! Don't we all suffer from 'empty nest' syndrome?" This was the first time we'd been apart so it was understandable. After she disappeared inside her new home, Doug and I sat outside in the van while I wept rivers of tears onto the shoulders of his best suit jacket.

Kecia's major was Microbiology. Her studies involved many weekends of field work which kept her away from home for long periods of time. Keeping busy helped to pass the time but the truth was that Doug was also missing Kecia. To our delight, she came home for the summer holidays and our home was happy once again. This was the way it would be until her four years of study were complete.

After she completed her second year of university, Kecia helped me to establish a chapter for the American Diabetes Association. Being severely ill off and on with my own diabetes, I wanted to give back so that others could benefit from the services of this wonderful organization. To kick off our grand opening, we'd been granted permission from the US Navy to conduct the first ever 'Walk on Water' event through Bremerton with celebrations held on the USS Carl Vinson. It was an astounding success and surely one for the local history books. Kecia joined a dance troop under the direction of Felix Fabellano and danced her heart out on the decks of that grand ship to entertain the crowds. We went all out for that event with prizes, t-shirts, food and lots of entertainment. It was a great honor when Governor Norm Dicks kicked off our first official walk and Dr. Todd Schneiderman helped me to MC the event. This was the first of many walks with Kecia and everyone who helped to make our annual walk memorable. I lived for those times when we would spend such quality time together and I never forgot for a moment that God had blessed me with the most perfect daughter in the world.

After three years of putting up with my parents, we made the difficult decision to close the store. Business had been suffering due to mother's antics and I was just plain sick and tired of her bossiness. According to her, she ran the show and expected us to jump through hoops to meet her demands. Keeping the display cabinets stocked was her job but she outright refused to do it, calling it 'menial' work. When I reminded her that it was her responsibility, she'd give me her stock reply, "Stop complaining and just get it done!" Our biggest concern was our losses. We supplied thirty-three truffle recipes and she was giving them away by the box load to her family and friends as though it were her decision to make. When J. Watson came to town, she sent each of his family members off with a one pound box. In true 'grande dame' fashion, she even pretended to be 'Mamie' to our customers and didn't miss a beat when it came to issuing orders to me in their presence. "I think customers knew what was going on, especially when I'd give them my tell-all wink and a smile." That never sat well with mother, who would then accuse me of embarrassing her in front of 'her' customers.

Life settled down after that and I enjoyed having peace back in my life. Mind you, that didn't stop mother from interfering every chance she got. Around that time, J. Watson separated from his wife and there was mother, chomping at the bit to choose his next one for him. She even encouraged him to strike up a special friendship with her neighbor, Teresa. Well, I guess he did because one thing led to another and the two of them had a son together and they named him Conrad. He was such a beautiful child and mother doted on him, much the same way that she had with J. Watson. If I didn't know better, history was repeating itself. Mother used

Conrad to torment me every chance she got, much the same way she did when I was a child.

Both mother and I were doll collectors and none of the children in the family were allowed to handle them, not ever. They could look but not touch. These were expensive dolls...the kind that are kept in secure cabinets because of their value. My love for dolls had carried over from childhood and at one time, I had built a business, importing dolls from around the world and wholesaled them to fine retail stores. Many of the fine dolls in her cabinet were actually gifts from me.

I recall the time when I caught Conrad playing with one of mother's most expensive collector dolls. Mother didn't seem to mind or pay much attention. When I asked him to put it back, all she said was, "Leave him alone! He's just a little boy and I'll decide what he can play with, not you!" I suppose it all goes back to her cultural theory that boys should be more privileged than girls because she never would have allowed that with Kecia when she was growing up. She went on to tell me that she was babysitting Conrad because his mama had just undergone a brain procedure that morning and was resting in the bedroom. Well, that was a first...my mother babysitting!

It was easy to see that Conrad was very spoiled and willful. The doll was one that I had given to her and it didn't even faze her that he was ripping its arms off and pulling its hair. When I saw that, I was enraged that she didn't even try to stop him. I told him to put that doll down and explained to him that it was not a toy. He replied, "No!" When I repeated my instruction, he screamed back at me, "Shut up!" Mother's only response was to try to shush me up, telling me, "Be quiet! My daughter's in the next room and she's trying to rest!" Well, that did it! I went at her with all guns ablaze!

"In the first place, Teresa is not your daughter! She's nothing to you, not even your daughter-in-law!" And I didn't stop there. "She's just a neighbor who's trying to destroy J. Watson's marriage and she's doing it with your help! What's the matter with you mother?"

She flew into a rage and screamed at me to get out of her house. As I was leaving, she shouted after me, "My daughter and grandson mean more to me than you ever did! You were always jealous of J. Watson and now you're jealous of my new daughter and her son!" I could hear little Conrad in the background. "Grandma hates you and she wants you to get out. I hate you too!" Before I could even get out the door, she lunged at me like a mad woman and grabbed me by the hair and shoved me against the door frame. Her final words stung the most. "You just don't get it. I've always been able to find others to replace you. Now just get out and don't ever come back!" That's when I gave her my final shot. "Teresa's nothing but a gold digger so you'd better watch your back mother!" Then she shoved me out the door with a kick to my back. "Oh, did I tell you the part where my father just stood there didn't try to stop her…no surprise there!"

Six months went by without a word from either mother or dad. His silence hurt the most as he could at least have called when she was out shopping but he never did. So much for our little secret. He used to tell me when I was little that I was his favorite but I was never to tell Mother that.

Then right out of the blue, mother called as if nothing had ever happened and without even so much as an apology. Like a love starved child, I still missed her and longed for her love when we were apart. So, like a little lost sheep, I went running back. My parents had moved here when no one else wanted them, yet all we ever got from them was aggravation and grief. Our finances and our physical and emotional health took a beating because of them. The only reason Doug and Kecia endured mother's crap was out of love for me because they knew that I couldn't bring myself to give up on her. Kecia and I meant no more to her than pieces of gravel on the road that you kick around when you have nothing better to do.

It didn't take long to realize that my parents had fallen upon hard times and that's why they came calling again. They knew that we'd always be there for them no matter what! J. Watson was well off financially and he gave generously to them but it was never enough. My parents were aging and at the end of the day, they were my family and I couldn't bring myself to abandon them.

19

Sweet Memories

Vacation of a Lifetime-Ireland

"When I awoke this morning, I began to record some of my fondest memories to share with you." I don't have many from my earlier years but I hope to show that it really is possible to change your destiny to one of achievement and happiness if only you determine to never give up.

ABOUT GANELLE...

My first grand memory is about my best friend, Ganelle Swanson. "I must be careful in describing our friendship so that you'll understand why she was so special in my life."

I'd been working as a cocktail waitress making good tips, but I yearned for something more prestigious with the opportunity to work my way up the ladder. That's when I interviewed for an office position at a large hotel. I figured that my experience working for my Aunt Elaine was good preparation and anything that I didn't know, I could fudge my way through to get the job. I needed this job desperately and so I showed up in my most conservative office attire. Was I ever glad that I did because the other women who showed up for interviews were anything but modestly dressed. It was apparent by the way the manager looked these women up and down, that he might have had ulterior motives. That worried me because I was not the most voluptuous or attractive candidate and so I determined to wow him with my skills.

By the time it was my turn, I was trembling inside and hoped that it wouldn't show. Well, I did just fine in the interview and I told him that I was willing to learn new skills if he'd only give me the chance. He was impressed that I knew so much about the business at such a young age and approved me for a second interview with his office manager who would make the final decision. Her name was Ganelle, a vibrant woman about five foot four with brown hair and eyes. Her smile lit up the room, and I got the feeling that this was one woman who had the wherewithal to size me up quickly.

She took me to the coffee shop inside the hotel and we talked for what seemed like hours over lunch, as she got to know me. I must have put my best foot forward because I got the job. At the end of our meeting, Ganelle made one savvy remark that stuck with me. "Always appear confident and positive and no one will ever know what you might be holding back." That was her way of telling me that she knew I wasn't fully qualified but had faith in me anyway.

"By now, you know that I've never been daunted by hard work." I put in endless hours, off the clock, to learn new credentials so that I could work my way up in the organization. It wasn't long before I had learned every aspect of banquet management and hotel bookkeeping. Ganelle gave me every opportunity to advance and I can't tell you how much I respected her for believing in me.

In time, we became fast friends. We had so much in common and got along famously. At work, she treated me like a professional but outside, as a true friend. Ganelle understood that life should not be all about work and that play was a necessary element of a well-rounded person. We began to spend our spare time at the beach together, searching for those mysterious glass floats from Japan that would show up occasionally on the water. I learned the relaxing thrill of beach combing on those wonderful outings. In no time, the Oregon coast became our playground where we enjoyed the aquarium and even the bumper cars. "Who said that bumper cars were only for kids anyway?" After a few hours of relaxation, we'd head back and stop in at The Gingerbread House on the way home for coffee and dessert. Occasionally, we stayed overnight at the beach in search of fresh Dungeness crab to take home. Those days were reminiscent of my time with Colena who taught me how to cook them just right.

While I loved my job, it wasn't long before the Manager let it be known that he had other plans in mind for me. My first instinct had been right about him and I found myself looking over my shoulder just to avoid him. Because of his incessant pestering, it became necessary for me to move on and find work elsewhere and so I took my new skills and headed to the hotel right next door. It was part of a large, well known chain and represented a step up in my career path. I had come to them well qualified, thanks to the excellent tutelage of my good friend, Ganelle.

We were only next door from one another and so it was easy to keep up our friendship. We spoke often and joined one another for dinner after work at least two or three times a week. As a true friend, she continued to encourage me. Her best advice was, "Never give up and always reach for the sky!"

My new job turned out to be more of a challenge that I'd expected. At first I dreaded that I might be in over my head when I found out that I was responsible for overseeing the front desk and housekeeping, restaurant management, bookkeeping and get this—payroll for hundreds of employees. "What had I gotten myself into?" I was back to taking work home every night with Ganelle tutoring me in the areas that I still needed to learn. In no time, I was seeing the results of my persistence and I became the professional that I'd always longed to be. I was happy in that job and stayed for a good long time. I must confess that I secretly wondered if mother would be proud of me, now that I was a success in the business world.

Many years later, I moved away to Washington State but Ganelle remained my dearest friend and beach combing buddy. We visited often and maintained our friendship for over forty years. She would later lose her beloved husband and her son, forcing her to endure the saddest time in her life. This only drew us closer and, like sisters, we stuck together through thick and thin.

After her loss, Ganelle moved to Springfield, Oregon where she opened up her own floral business. She had studied the art of floral design and combined with her aptitude for management, she had that business flourishing in no time at all. Most of her time was spent working and so it wasn't surprising that we weren't able to spend as much time together as we had become accustomed to. Before we knew it, a few years had elapsed before the next opportunity would come along. That special occasion turned out to be my wedding day—an event that she would not have missed for the world.

I wanted that special day to become a picture perfect memory but to save money, I took on many of the preparations on my own. I even took on the task of making my own floral arrangements. "Well, that was the plan anyway and we all know what a good planner I was!" I ended up spending three times what it would have cost to have them done professionally. I wasn't even close to having them done and the day was fast approaching. Enter Ganelle! She arrived a couple of days early and picked up the pieces to save the day. The arrangements were stunning but I couldn't take much credit for that. I had only finished the corsages and boutonnieres and had barely started on the arrangements for the altar let alone the pieces that would adorn the pews.

It would be several more years before Doug and I travelled to Oregon to spend a couple of weeks with my dear friend. We spent good quality time together, doing the things that we loved the most, especially at the beach. For a long time, Ganelle had been gently nudging me to sit down and write this book. I would work at it now and again but never seemed to make any real progress because it was just too painful and difficult to dredge up my childhood memories. On this visit, Ganelle urged me to sit down and try again and so I wrote, late into each night after she went to bed. She proofread my notes every morning over breakfast and never forgot to encourage me to stay at it. It seemed easier with her being so near and for the first time, I made some serious headway with my story.

This was the beginning of my fourteen year crusade to complete this labor of love but it wasn't until sixteen years had elapsed that I committed to finishing it, in part as a tribute to her memory. A good friend will always tell you the truth and it was she who had told me, "Mamie, you'll never completely heal until this work is done. Never give up!"

Ganelle and I had so many great times together and it's hard to pick only a few to share with you. One of those times was our visit to a huge shopping mecca on the coast in Lincoln City…and shop we did. Instead of making a couple of trips to the car to relieve ourselves of our purchases, we shopped merrily away, until we had far too much for two people to carry. "If you happened to notice two women, one walking with a cane, dragging at least a dozen bags across the parking lot in search of their car, that was Ganelle and I." We'd shopped non-stop…bedspreads, linens, clothes, suitcases and you name it, but we couldn't find the darned car! Finally, we gave up, too exhausted to take another step and literally sat down on a curb, unable to stop laughing at ourselves. Apparently, we'd been entertaining others as well because a young couple took pity on us and carried our bags while we searched for our car.

On my last visit with Ganelle, we decided to attend the Lane County Fair to check out the new merchandise for the season. We hadn't made it past the front lobby when we were greeted by the most heavenly piano music I'd ever listened to. We were spellbound by the serenity of the soothing melodies and stopped to enjoy the entire performance. Ganelle had been fighting an aggressive form of cancer and I was going through a particularly difficult time with my diabetes yet we both experienced the same calming sensation as we soaked in that beautiful music. The pianist was none other than the one and only Charles Suniga of 'Moments of Peace' fame. I still listen to his music whenever I feel the need to relax. Indeed, whenever I was struggling to resurrect the horrific details of a particular abuse episode for this book, it was Charles playing in the background who helped me to face my demons and heal my heavy heart.

HAWAII – OUR DREAM TRIP!

Another precious memory that I'd like to share is our dream vacation to Hawaii. We chose that beautiful location to meld as a new family unit, so only Doug, Kecia and I got to enjoy this one. We pulled out all the stops—first class all the way! When we landed in Honolulu, we checked into the **Sheraton Moana Surfrider**, a palace of a resort that boasted the pinkest sand beaches I'd ever seen. Only the pink tinted buildings with their huge welcoming columns came anywhere near to emulating the delicate tint of that sand.

Talk about paradise! The food was delectable and our suite was pure luxury. We toured all of the popular sites on the island, and even hopped over to Kauai to take in its beauty. Especially enjoyable was our visit to the sugar plantation. I had fantasized about slurping that fresh pure sugar straight from the cane and I can tell you, I was not disappointed.

Kauai was not the bustling tourist destination that I expected it would be. It was better known for its beauty and pristine beaches that fairly gleamed from the sparkling reflection of the ocean. I loved the tranquility but after a while, I yearned for the big island with its crowded beaches and festive Hawaiian dinner entertainment.

No Hawaiian adventure would be complete without a trek to Diamond Head and so we set out in a group to explore its many wonders. That hike was an eye opener for us all, but especially me. It was terribly hot and the walk was exhausting. Still somewhat in denial about my diabetes, I had brought along my testing supplies but left my insulin behind, a foolish oversight if there ever was one. By the time we completed the climb, I knew that something was terribly wrong and looked forward to some time out to rest but I was determined to complete the tour with Kecia and Doug. The view from the top was, without question, one of the most spectacular scenes on God's green earth. It was hard to imagine anyone diving from those lofty cliffs as I had seen in the movies. It was another seven-hundred foot trek to the top of the crater with its surprising views of Waikiki and Oahu's south shore.

I must say that I was happy when we were back on the tour bus. At least I was able to rest up for the next activity and avoid the hot sun for a while. My time out came when Doug and Kecia went snorkeling. Doug had served in the Navy so deep sea diving and snorkeling were second nature to him. Kecia begged me, "Please Mom, let me go too!" So off they went, hand in hand to explore the wonders of the sea bottom, or so I thought. As much as I loved the ocean, I always stayed close to shore where I could still see the bottom but not them. They ventured out way beyond the best snorkeling grounds until they were barely visible. I was beginning to feel anxious once I could no longer spot them. They must have been underwater because when they emerged, I realized that my wonderful husband had everything under control and would never put my daughter in any danger.

Though snorkeling wasn't my thing, Doug and Kecia had a great time and returned cool and refreshed, ready for whatever came next. I learned an important lesson that day…just let go and believe that Doug would never fail me. From that day forward, I trusted him with our lives.

When we got back to our suite, I tested my blood sugar. My numbers were soaring and I needed multiple doses of insulin to get it back to a safe level. I couldn't believe that I had risked my health because I didn't take it seriously enough to take the necessary precautions. From that day on, wherever I went, my insulin went too.

Once I was feeling better, we readied ourselves for a magnificent evening at the Polynesian Cultural Center, about an hour's drive from our hotel. As we entered, we were presented with traditional orchid leis, our second on this trip, and then sat down to enjoy a meal that was fit for royalty. We even joined the dancers on stage to learn the traditional dances of the Hawaiian and South Pacific cultures. This magical evening culminated in a Polynesian night show and an authentic luau. "Oh how we wished it would never end!"

On a more sober note, we made it a point to visit the Pearl Harbor memorial and gave our silent tribute to all of those young men who had lost their lives on that fateful day in 1945.

Back at the hotel, Doug insisted that I check my blood sugar and once again, the reading came back HIGH! This was happening too often and Doug decided to take matters into his own hands, swearing that it would never happen again on his watch. I already mentioned that he had made it a point to learn everything there was to know about this dreadful disease and because of him, I would never again take it for granted.

All in all, this trip cemented our family bond and we knew that nothing would ever come between us.

WHISTLER – A MAGICAL CHRISTMAS!

Whistler Village Center is the hub of activity in this snow blanketed mountain paradise, where tourists ski by day and enjoy a mass of twinkling lights and entertainment by night! Planning our winter getaway was such a joy. We'd be celebrating Christmas; therefore, it was important to pay a lot of attention to detail so that the atmosphere would be just right. I reserved our lodging inside the square, just a few minutes' walk from the ski lift. Knowing that we wouldn't have a tree at home that year, I phoned ahead to order a huge display of poinsettia plants for our suite. Finally, I spent many hours wrapping our gifts in beautiful papers and huge decorative bows. I was already sentimental and we weren't even there yet!

We were all delighted with our two bedroom suite. We unpacked and Kecia set up a comfy little area for Coco, her little puppy. Gorgeous red poinsettia plants were everywhere and by the time I laid out our gift packages, the Christmas atmosphere was warm and inviting.

Our main gift for Kecia was her ski lift tickets and did she ever make good use of them. She whooshed down those slopes for hours on end while I was busy trying to catch a glimpse of her so that I could snap some pictures. It was good to see her happy and give her this break from everyday life.

I discovered early on that Doug was one who loved to please and I was no different. A typical conversation would go like this:

Doug: Dear, what would you like to do today?
Me: I really don't care honey, whatever you like.
Doug: No, let's do whatever you want.

Well, that was all well and good but often we'd just spend our day trying to make each other happy, but not this time! This was no ordinary occasion. I had pre-booked so many activities that all he had to do was show up. And so our adventures began!

I had always imagined how romantic it would be to ride in a horse drawn carriage through the night snow under a moonlit sky…you know, a sleigh ride of sorts. Add Christmas caroling in an old fashioned barn and you have enough nostalgia to write a book about. Well, that's exactly what we did. I never gave a second thought that those horses were hitched up after their dinner feed of hay and were ready to drop roses on anyone who just happened to be sitting in the front seats. You needed to be there to appreciate the harmony… us singing Christmas carols and the horses expressing their musical opinions.

Our last outing was an evening snowmobile ride to the top of Black Comb Mountain. Wow! In my wildest dreams, I would never have imagined myself tracking up those slopes with sheer drop-offs on either side. Kecia rode on the back of the tour leader's machine and I rode with Doug. Jeepers, was it ever cold! It would all be worth it though. When we reached the top, we pulled up in front of a mountain lodge and went inside. We were greeted by a roaring fire and served wine, hot chocolate and warm appetizers. When we had warmed up, we headed back down the mountain. "Now, I'm not saying that the ride back down wasn't just as scary, because it was!"

As you can see, our family was built on a strong foundation of undeniable love, and nothing would ever take that away from us. You see, dreams really do come true if you never give up! But that's not all! I saved the sweetest memory of all to the last.

KECIA'S WEDDING

Now, I'd like to share a major milestone in Kecia's life. She had met that one special man who she wanted to spend the rest of her life with. When she brought him home to meet us, I can't begin to tell you how impressed we were. Jonathan was his name and he was serving in the Navy. He was the perfect match for our daughter... tall and handsome, quiet, compassionate and very polite. In fact, his manners were impeccable when he asked Doug for our daughter's hand in marriage. Oh yes, I had dreamt about that day for such a long time but now that it was here, the reality set in that she would be moving on without me. "How could I be so happy for her yet so sad at the same time?"

A wonderful flurry of activity filled our days as arrangements were being made for her big event. Naturally, I did all of the motherly things to prepare my sweet daughter for the biggest walk of her life. We shopped, attended wedding showers and honored all of the traditions befitting such a special occasion.

Ganelle was still with us at that time and was a special part of the wedding. She was Kecia's Godmother and it wouldn't have been the same without her. I spent two weeks with her well in advance of the wedding to work on the floral decorations. We spent nearly every waking hour creating sixty pew bows with matching sprays and table decorations, all with gorgeous ribbon and ivy. Fresh flowers would be added to each piece at the last minute. We howled with laughter each day as we shared old memories and made some new ones. When I was leaving, she promised to come a few days early to help out with last minute arrangements.

When the big day finally arrived, I silently prayed that their love would last forever and that they would be as happy as Doug and I were. As I helped Kecia into her wedding gown, I was overcome with emotion. She was the epitome of perfection and my heart overflowed with pride.

"Have you ever seen a fairy princess in a flowing white gown?" That was Kecia as her proud daddy walked her down the aisle to join hands with her handsome young prince who awaited her at the altar. Once they were pronounced man and wife, I began to breathe again. Their union was blessed and it was time to hand over the reins to Jonathan.

After the reception, the happy couple said their goodbyes and left to enjoy their honeymoon. They would be leaving the next day on a luxury cruise. Kecia must have known that I would miss them terribly and decided to surprise us with a telephone call from the dock before they boarded their ship.

I felt that I had come full circle, beginning with my perfect wedding and now Kecia's. Yes, life was good and all because I listened to Ganelle who reminded me again that I should never give up!

20

Tributes & Farewells

Our family as we began

"Friends, I ask that you walk with me as I pay tribute to my significant family and friends who left too soon." Through good times and bad, through thick and thin, I am connected to them for eternity and it makes me feel whole and healthy to share this with you.

IN MEMORY OF MY MOTHER

I lost my mother on February 20th, 2004.

My struggles never ended with her and I'll never know for sure if she ever felt remorse over her failure to bond with me, her only daughter. I only know that my need for her love persisted to the very end while I continued to stand by her side despite our differences.

My mother had diverticulitis and had lost most of her stomach and intestines to this progressive disease. It was suspected, but never proven, that she may also have had cancer. She suffered for many years with her ailments and I suppose that it all just caught up with her in the end.

We brought her into our home for the last six months of her life. Papa had been gone for three and a half years and I needed to know that she was well taken care of, even it meant that I'd be biting my tongue most of the time. Though I had put our differences aside, mother continued to make my life a living hell and demanded that I wait on her hand and foot. It mattered little what time of the day or night; if she wanted something, she ordered me to get it for her and for the life of me, I didn't know how to refuse. At that time she was perfectly capable of taking care of her own personal needs, but she preferred to have her own hand maiden to do her bidding. When I found out that she was spreading lies to her friends about us, that we were abusing her and lying about her, we were terribly hurt. If all of this behavior had begun in her later years, I might have had her diagnosed for age related illness but she had been that way all of her life.

Mother's demands took a serious toll on my own health. When I was still recovering from double hip surgery to remove damaged areas caused by my arthritis, the added strain of chasing after her and suffering her continuous verbal abuse was almost more than I could bear. I suppose she couldn't stop herself but when she hurled her nasty insults at Doug, I drew the line and let her know it. My stress level was so severe that my weight dropped dramatically and my dress size went down from a size ten to a four. But when my blood sugar got out of control, that's when my husband dug in his heels and said enough is enough.

Despite the stress, we took mother everywhere with us rather than leaving her alone to fare for herself. It was almost a break to do so because somehow, she would experience a miraculous recovery whenever we did the things she wanted to do.

On one occasion, Ganelle joined us for a short vacation at the beach. Mother adored the seashore so that was something that we all had in common. Doug and I rented a beach house with all the creature comforts and we settled in to enjoy our vacation. Mother seemed in pretty good shape when we left, having just recovered from another bad episode of her illness.

On the first day, we enjoyed a leisurely walk on the beach and after a wonderful dinner, sat and watched the sea for what seemed like hours before calling it a night. We slept in the next morning and decided to take it slow before venturing out for the day's activities. After enjoying a hearty brunch, we set off for the gift shop to see what it had to offer. The route to the shops was lined with attractive beach homes and we all took turns oh'ing and aw'ing at any that caught our fancy. Mother, being her usually pretentious self, piped in that she was thinking about buying our beach house. It didn't even occur to her that it belonged to a resort but she was enjoying herself and so I let it go by. By the time we got back it was raining, forcing us to stay indoors for the rest of the day.

During the night, mother called out my name and I raced to her room. I didn't like her color or the weakness in her voice when she spoke, "Mamie, I don't feel too good." I asked if she wanted to go to the hospital but she assured me that she just needed to sleep for a while and would see how she felt in the morning. And so I tucked her in, kissed her goodnight and tried to get back to sleep but there would be no more sleep for me that night. Something in her voice frightened me and I didn't want to leave her alone. Ganelle joined me and we laid next to her to keep watch.

By dawn, mother's condition had worsened. There was a certain knowing in her eyes as she told me, "I'm going to die today." Doug beckoned help from the front desk and an ambulance was dispatched immediately. I stayed by her side and held her hand while we waited for the ambulance to arrive. I had never seen my mother in a helpless state before and it was quite alarming. By the time the ambulance got there, she had already slipped into a coma. Doug and Ganelle rushed to pack up the van, while I rode with mother in the ambulance, begging her to open her eyes and to stay with me.

Ganelle joined me at the hospital while Doug rushed home to unload the van and drop off the trailer. It was a lengthy round trip but it felt so good to have him back by my side to help me through this saddest of times. I put calls through to J. Watson and Herb and urged them to hurry if they wanted to see mother again while there was still time. The next day, J. Watson flew out to Seattle and picked up Kecia to drive together to the hospital. She came to be with me and put her differences with her grandmother aside. Mother had never welcomed her as her own, more because she was my daughter than for any other reason. After a good deal of soul searching, Herb decided to stay away. His relationship with her was hopelessly broken and they never were able to reconcile. Because she had failed us completely as a mother, he felt no desire to be with her at the end. I completely understood how difficult it was for him.

Ganelle joined Doug and I at mother's bedside while she was undergoing a battery of tests and being medicated through an IV drip. I spent that night trying to come to terms with losing her. I must have asked myself a thousand times why my tears kept falling despite our tragic history of abuse and then it came to me. I loved my mother deeply and never did stop hoping that someday, she would love me back. Well, now it was 'someday' and I was on edge knowing that time was running out.

On the second day, Kecia and J. Watson arrived at the hospital. Just minutes before, the doctor removed her IV, after explaining that there was nothing more they could do to save her. The best thing we could do was to keep the vigil until she was ready to let go. Another night went by and mother was still hanging on. I wondered if she was going to recover after all or if she was waiting for Herb. Could it be that she was ready to make peace before it was too late? Oh, how I hoped that was the case.

Because there was nothing more they could do to help her, we made arrangements to bring mother home to spend her remaining time with family. Doug and Ganelle got a head start to prepare the house for her homecoming. Doug arranged for oxygen to be delivered and started a blazing hot fire in the family room to keep her comfortable and warm. Mother had always complained that her hands were cold and it was so like Doug to go out of his way to make her remaining time as comfortable as possible. I rode with her in the ambulance while J. Watson and Kecia followed behind. Once the oxygen supply was setup at home, the medical team moved her in on a stretcher and lifted her onto the comfortable lounge chair that Doug had prepared for her. Then they covered her with warm blankets, where she would stay until the end. Before leaving, the team checked her oxygen supply and determined that she needed a good deal more. After it was delivered, our final vigil began.

J. Watson sat up all night singing songs to her. One of her favorites was *Willie Nelson's On the Road Again* and it still hurts my heart whenever I hear it. Sitting next to the warm fire made me sleepy and I went to my bedroom to rest for a while. After about an hour,

Ganelle came to wake me. She spoke softly in my ear, "Come now Mamie. I think it's time."

I hurried to her side, all the while praying to God that, "If we're ever to make things right between us, please let it be now." I needed her to apologize before it was too late. I leaned over and whispered the words, "I love you mommy. Please love me back." Then I kissed her goodbye and as she drew her last breath, a single tear ran down her cheek.

"I will tell you this my friends. Mother never did confess to loving me but l choose to believe that this was a tear of regret."

IN MEMORY OF MY PAPA

My papa left us on October 20th, 2000.

He was an adult onset diabetic who didn't manage his disease very well. Many years of neglect took a serious toll on his health and by the time he was well into his senior years, he was already suffering through many life threatening illnesses.

I'm taken back to Christmas of 1992, when we were in the candy business. We were exhibiting our chocolates at the Kitsap Christmas Gourmet show, a prestigious event located in the mall. Exhibitors dressed in elegant evening wear, to suit the ballroom theme of the show. We were thrilled to have papa work the booth with us and I must say that he did look dapper in his formal attire.

Everything was going along smoothly until he suddenly took ill. It happened over dinner. At one point I turned toward him and noticed that he was staring off into space. His hand was clenched tightly onto his plate, as though he had a death grip on it. Something was seriously wrong and an ambulance was called immediately. In the meantime, I tried to wrestle the plate out of his hands while shouting, "Papa, let go of the plate! If you're hungry, I'll feed you. Just let go!" I don't know if he realized what was happening because he suddenly wandered off and tried to leave. "Papa!" I yelled to get his attention. "Stop where you are and come back!" When we got him back to the table, Doug kept reassuring him, "Jack, just sit here and we'll take care of you. We love you." We had to restrain him in the booth until medical help finally arrived.

He had suffered a major stroke and had to undergo Carotid Artery surgery. After that, he was never the same. I had studied and worked with patients suffering stroke effects so I recognized his symptoms, crying out "dear God, please spare my papa." The stroke had taken a serious toll on his health and his stamina never did return to normal, although he tried his best to keep up. When he recovered, he said to me "I love you and I'm so grateful you were there for me when it all happened. I was so afraid." Between hospital visits and having to keep the store operating, with only Doug to help me out, it was a strain to say the least. After working a full shift at his government job, he spent nearly every waking hour helping me through this busiest season of the year. I needed to hire extra help but mother gave us so much grief about it, we had to go it alone. We had hired Kecia and her friend for the season but mother made it a point to warn me, "If you pay them for helping, it had better come out of your own pocket. Kecia owes us so she won't get a cent from me."

The next year was even worse. Papa suffered several heart attacks and underwent a quadruple by-pass operation that meant a lengthy recovery at home. Again, Doug and I found ourselves alone during the busy Christmas season. By this time, papa no longer needed constant care and so we were counting on mother to back us up in the store but that's not the way it happened! Being the proverbial 'arm chair critic', she preferred to give her 'expert' direction from her recliner chair at home and there wasn't anything that I could say or do to change her mind. That was strange because mother was never willing to get her own hands dirty, complaining, "That's your thing and I'll deal with the customers." Despite her absence, we enjoyed our most successful season yet. We had made it through with twenty hour days and the welcome help from Kecia and her friend who were home from college for the holidays. By Christmas Eve morning, our shelves were bare and we lacked the energy to replenish them. We decided to close the store for the holidays and get some much needed rest.

Eventually, papa recovered well enough to come back to the store and it did my heart good to have him there. He managed to work the full year and he truly did his best to be useful in any way he could. Mother was a different story and I simply tired of carrying her weight as well as my own and so we shut our doors for the last time in January 1995.

Over the next few years, papa's health continued to go downhill, mostly from diabetic issues. It truly hurt to see him suffer so badly but he was paying the price for having neglected his health for too many years. In the end, his right leg was amputated and two days after that, he choked to death in a coughing episode. Mother blamed me because I had taken a photo of him the day before. According to her, papa was superstitious about taking photographs in hospitals. I stayed with his body until they removed him from his room. Distraught, I laid across his chest and wept, "Oh papa, I'm so sorry that you died without your family by your side. Please forgive me for taking that photograph. I didn't mean for you to die."

Now, when I think of him, I choose to remember the time we spent together in the beach house when we lived in Houston. Sure, he had let Herb and I down as a father but he made up for it when he was separated from mother. I had never felt such peace and hoped that it never end. As it turned out, that time was brief but I'll cherish it forever.

FAREWELL MY DEAR FRIEND - GANELLE

Ganelle passed away from cancer in 2010, leaving behind sweet memories of a beautiful friendship. I know first-hand that she watches over me as my guardian angel in times of need. I even experienced her presence when I was struggling through a life and death experience due to the complications of diabetes. "I miss you my sweet friend. You were another who made me promise to never give up!" *(for more information, see chapter 19).*

FAREWELL DEAR TONY

In 1985 I had the honor of meeting and becoming close friends with Tony Lang. We were first introduced in a job interview for the position of Encephalographer Trainee. Tony was a disciplined professional and a tough trainer but thanks to him, I made the grade. He had made it clear that he wanted me to be the best that I could be before he could recommend me to the Neurologist in my area. Indeed, I have him to thank for being established in a good paying profession, enabling me to support my little girl as a single parent.

Tony was a wonderful support for Kecia and even became her Godfather and a committed family friend. When he met and married his lovely wife, Catherine I couldn't have been happier for him. To this day, Catherine remains a cherished friend.

Thank you Tony for giving me a chance to prove myself and for becoming a special part of my family. My life has been greatly enriched
for having known you. Tony passed away on October 13th, 2006.

FAREWELL, OUR SWEET SANDY

Sandy Adkins
May 11, 2002 to March 22, 2013

Silence, heartbreak and emptiness greeted us as we unlocked the door to our home that night. Our dearest friend and family member had moved on without us. Her spirit was not strong enough to survive another day and at 5:30 P.M., March 22, 2013, our world was shattered as we watched her pass on to a healthier place.

Sandy, our wonderful, sweet chocolate Labrador Retriever, had a heart of pure gold. She never complained if she was sick or hurt, was loyal to everyone she loved and was smart in every way. Sandy had filled our lives for nearly eleven years and now she was gone and our house was empty. It wasn't until she left when we finally understood how so much of the peaceful, loving atmosphere in our home was because of her. Each May, Doug and Sandy had celebrated their birthdays together, having been born on the same day.

Sandy earned her name when we first brought her home because her very first stroll was on the beach. The seashore had always been a peaceful, playful haven for me and so it was for Sandy. Splashing in the water, digging in the sand and of course, exploring whatever she found in the washed up seaweed! She raced up and down the beach for hours on end as though her energy was boundless. This was her game and it was for Doug and I to keep up.

As she grew a bit older and graduated from her playpen, she earned her stripes by chewing up the remotes for our adjustable beds. Naturally we had to order replacements but had to cope with our beds stuck in awkward positions for several days while we waited for the new ones to arrive.

Before Sandy, we had always had poodles so it was up to her to train us in her own unique way. Knowing that she would was going to be a very large dog, she was not allowed to get onto the bed at night—at least that was the plan. Sandy had other ideas! When her playpen failed to contain her, Doug and I headed off to the pet store in search of other options. We bought an outdoor fence and encircled our bed with it, knowing that we had finally solved the problem or so we thought. When we'd open our eyes in the morning, there she'd be, either staring us in the face or curled up fast asleep against our chest or legs. Once we lost that battle, Sandy became a regular in our bed, taking up ever more room as she grew from what we thought would be forty-five pounds to more than a hundred. Her independence and drive seemed to be saying, "Never give up," as though she knew how I had lived my entire life.

Sandy loved us very much and expressed it through her daily routines. One of her daily habits was to greet each sunrise through the glass doors in our bedroom. She'd push the vertical blinds aside with her nose and gently wake us up, as if to say, "Good morning, the sun's up." That was Doug's cue to hang his leg over the side of the bed and gently rub her tummy as she wrapped her paws around his foot.

When the time came for our young 'child' to attend obedience school, we fully expected she'd have her PhD in obedience in no time flat. Well, she didn't but she was a good teacher. We learned to take walks, Sandy style, eat while she tilted her sweet head as if to ask, "Where's my plate?" and watch the TV programs that she most enjoyed.

Our lives with Sandy were filled with endless laughter and delight, though there were some frustrating times as well. Sandy knew that it was her job to protect us and our home which was her property too. No one would ever dare enter our home with the intention of harming any of her people. She had a bark that would set anyone on notice but if she knew that our guests were invited, she would simply form a circle with her mouth and 'woooo' in her soft voice, as if to say hello and welcome to her home.

Sandy's life wasn't easy, medically speaking. She suffered from seizures and allergies. When it came to her weight, I'm sure that her feelings were hurt when people laughed or remarked that she was fat. Little did they know that she was suffering from a thyroid problem. We protected her against such remarks but I'm sure that she understood and still responded lovingly with her beautiful sad eyes, wagging tail and soft kiss. Often, people are just too quick to judge without understanding the underlying cause and occasionally, such remarks simply lack compassion.

In her senior years, Sandy began to have issues with her feet which were misdiagnosed and blamed on her allergies. For the following two years, she endured allergy shots before she was correctly diagnosed with cancer. This resulted in surgical removal of half her foot and the need to learn to walk all over again. She never whined or complained about her obvious pain and frustration. Not our girl! She was determined to wear her bandages and socks with dignity and never give up.

Sandy's all time favorite thing was riding in the car. Her nick name should have been 'go' because whenever Doug or I spelled that word, the letter 'g' would no sooner be out of our mouth and she'd be heading for the door.

Age continued to take its toll on Sandy. When she developed bone spurs to the hips and knees, she was no longer able to enjoy the excitement of chasing squirrels but especially the long walks that we enjoyed together as a family. How she had loved it when we shook her leash, signaling that it was time for a walk but now she had to find other ways to enjoy her leisure time. The back deck became her favorite place to relax and take in the fresh air. Two little squirrels from our back yard made it a daily habit to scurry up to the deck as if to say, 'come play with us' causing her hair to stand up on end. Being the polite little soul that she was though, she still gently smiled back.

It was a special joy for Doug and I to defer to Sandy when she wanted to watch TV. She chose the shows that she wanted to watch and had her own way of letting us know what made her happy. She particularly liked shows with animals and made it a practice to chatter with them in her own language but if she didn't like eerie music, she'd be sure to express her opinion in no uncertain terms. Her front room bed faced the TV so she was able to watch her favorite programs.

It wasn't beyond Doug to sit on the floor with her and play their favorite game. Doug would take a treat and hold it in his fingers at Sandy's mouth and as she would go for it, he'd tuck it inside his palm. After repeating this a couple of times, Sandy would look away as if to say, "I don't want it anyway," but as soon as Doug looked away, she's run in with gusto and steal it away to win the game. To show her appreciation, she's wrap her little paws around his hand as if she'd never let go. This and so many games will be missed but remembered forever.

Although she wasn't well and often in discomfort, Sandy's last few days were especially difficult. She wasn't able to stand or walk on her own but believing that it was caused by her bone spurs, we expected it to be a temporary setback. Not satisfied, we sought a second opinion, hoping that our baby could be healed and become her happy and playful self again. Her earlier x-rays had revealed the bone spurs but there was never a mention that the major tendons in her knees were torn. Her new doctor told us that it was like having two broken legs that she would never recover from. He prescribed medication to treat the inflammation but explained that she wouldn't be able to walk for at least two to three weeks but wouldn't even promise that. Until she was well, she would need assistance going in and out but even if she recovered enough to walk again, he felt that we would be lucky to have her for another year.

On the way home from the vet's office, we stopped at a pet store to buy a sling. When I was leaving the store, Doug called out for me to hurry. I got to the car and saw that Sandy was struggling to breathe. We rushed back to the Vet's office and called ahead for them to expect us. When we got there, they were ready and waiting for us but it was too late. In spite of their efforts to revive her, Sandy just couldn't make this final journey.

Our hearts were full of grief wondering what we could have done differently. She had bled to death internally and we were helpless to do anything about it. She never complained even in her dying moments. God was merciful for taking her so quickly but we were in shock and disbelief because we hadn't expected it to be so soon. Our sweet baby of almost eleven years was finally at rest. We didn't sleep that night as we roamed the house, mourning her absence and not quite believing that she was actually gone.

Now each day is mixed with emotions as we remember the joy and laughter and finally, the sadness that Sandy brought to our lives. I know that she's in a good place and can run freely on the beach with the energy of a puppy. She can even chase that squirrel until she decides to let it escape as she always allowed it to do.

"Farewell sweet friend. We love you so. Be at peace and know that no other will ever take your place or replace the love that we shared with you. You are our angel now and we'll never forget you." Perhaps someday we'll love another but in a very different way.

This year, come May, Doug will celebrate his birthday without his special Sandy but you can be assured, she will be there in spirit and in our hearts.

IN MEMORY OF COCO, JENGER AND PIERRE

Our pets were so much a part of our family that they literally be-

came our children and don't think they didn't know it too. At one time, we had three poodles…Coco, Jenger and Pierre and we loved them all unconditionally. As you know, a pet is always loyal and your secrets are always safe with them.

Coco Channel was Kecia's baby apricot toy poodle. She was only six weeks old when we adopted her from a breeder. Oh, what a delight it was to present this little bundle of joy to her. Coco was so tiny that we wrapped her in a blanket like a newborn and surprised Kecia one day when we picked her up at elementary school.

Coco was a playful little thing and got a real kick out of sneaking up on you when you were least expecting it. She especially loved duel-ing with the cat and she'd use the same element of surprise to gain the advantage. When she grew up, she delivered a litter of puppies and remained a loving mother of Jenger and Pierre to the very end.

Coco joined the rest of the family for walks on the beach but she was always happiest when wrapped in a blanket, cuddled closely to Kecia's heart. Sadly, Coco passed away shortly after Kecia's fifteenth birthday.

Now **Jenger** was different in nature than her mother and spunky enough to reckon with other dogs, even if they towered over her in size. She was also an apricot but not as red as her mother. Her favor-  ite thing to do was play hide and seek. One day we returned home to find our little Houdini with her head stuck in- side a square Kleenex box. She was tearing around the room and bumping into walls as if she could bark her way out of that box. It was so like her to get herself into these strange predicaments. No doubt, she was the ham in the family and loved nothing better than to pose for the camera. A typical photo would be Jenger hiding behind a pillow with her little head peeking out as though to say, "Aren't I cute!" Her sweetest picture was taken on the stairs, wearing a wom- an's black hat with netting. She looked so smug in all her finery as if daring you to find anyone more gorgeous than her.

Like Coco and Pierre, she loved the beach but hated to get dirty. Her nick name was Little Miss Princess as she loved to be the belle of the ball in the presence of company.

Pierre had been a brave little soldier, taking his insulin faithfully each day and waiting for his prescribed snack. When I'd prepare our eve-

ning dinner, he loved to join me in the kitchen and position himself directly below the cutting board while I chopped and sliced vegetables. Naturally he was hoping that I'd drop a slice of tomato or another of his favourite foods and of course, I always did.

I wish you could have known this wonderful God given creature who taught me so many lessons. He stuck by my side through times of sadness and showered me with love and attention when I was very ill. This little sweetheart slept by my head at night and nudged me awake whenever he needed to be held like a baby. I still miss my little Pierre and always will.

Pierre was our darling baby boy, a childlike family member for nine years before we lost him. He suffered from the ravages of diabetes which brought about blindness and ultimately he bled to death.

21

Dreams Do Come True

Dublin

Kylemore Abbey

Ireland - West Coastline

Drifting off to sleep and then to reawaken to see my sweet adoring Douglas by my side was all it took to get me fantasizing. I thought about our wonderful life together and how to make it even better if that's possible. As I always do, I fell under the spell of his gentle smile and quiet blue eyes and counted my blessings for having him by my side. So now I ask you my dear friends, "How could I not want to share another journey with him?" Life just doesn't get much better than this and now, I have the most overwhelming urge to plan our next adventure!

Yes, this is me, doing what I have always done best…dream, plan and create life's most wonderful memories but this time, the word 'escape' will take on an entirely new meaning. Oh yes, this time I'll plan the grand-daddy of them all…an escape to a romantic location to celebrate our twenty-fifth wedding anniversary. Let's see now…I can't think of a better place to make our dream come true than to our magical fantasy land, the Emerald Isle.

Our first trip to Ireland was a dream come true where my precious husband and I renewed our wedding vows. That was in June 2011 and now, twenty-five years after we were first married, I can't think of a more fitting place to celebrate.

It's late February now and plans are now in full swing as we near the time when we return to Ireland in our hearts. To celebrate our anniversary and the release of my second book, *Reflections of Mamie*, I have invited some good friends to join us on our journey. Many plans have been made including book signings and visits to our favorite sites in that beautiful country.

I so want to share this journey with you but my book will be published months before the trip. So if you don't mind, I'll take you along now to share our fantasy vacation before it becomes a reality.

It's now late July and we're ready to embark on our magical vacation to Ireland. So please, let's travel to the lovely Emerald Island together with an advance trip to Scotland!

Our first stop will be at Edinburgh, Scotland where we'll visit Parliament for photo ops with the heads of state, followed by a rare guided tour of the government buildings. Next we'll move on to Edinburgh Castle and learn of its wonderful history. Just let your imagination transport you back in time to 900 BC when it was merely a fortress, where many battles were fought before it was captured and finally reconstructed as a castle in the year 1296. This monumental castle fills the skyline of Edinburgh and its massive size alone is more than a little bit intimidating.

Now we'll take a peak back in time to visualize the grandeur of the ladies of that period in long flowing gowns and the gentleman soldiers dressed in their finest. I can almost step into the role as *Julia Roberts* did in the movie, *Pretty Woman* when she was rescued by her knight in shining armor, played by *Richard Gere*…except that my knight is played by none other than my dashing husband, *Doug*. My gown would be made of pure white silk with a white overlay finished with hand crocheted roses and a trail that barely kisses the ballroom floor. Sir Douglas places his hand on my waist and with my hand gently on his shoulder, he would sweep me across the gleaming tiled ballroom floor in rhythm to the orchestra playing in the background.

Now let's move on to a little Scottish town named Fife. This is where our special friend, Jon Magee resides. Jon is the author of some very prestigious books, From *Barren Rocks to Living Stones, Paradise Island* and *Heavenly Journey*. http://www.lochgellybaptist@aol.com. Here we are introduced to true Scottish culture as Jon entertains us in his church with a festive Scottish dinner complete with Bagpipers and traditional dance.

The room spins with festive atmosphere as our friends gather around to begin the twenty-fifth anniversary celebration of our perfect marriage. It is all so precisely planned with song, laughter and fanfare which are beyond anything I could ever have imagined. Among our friends who are seated at our long banquet table are Jon and Joan Magee and my friend and editor, Linda Hales. Linda is an award winning author of *Andy-Roo: The Birthday Surprise!* Her newest title, *Sunshine and Her Big Blarney Smile!* was released in March 2013. Linda writes in a variety of genres but her special fondness is for children. See her website at http://www.linnieslittlebooks.com where amazon links are found. So, as you can see, our friends have their own reasons to celebrate as well.

Also at our table is Delinda McCann, author of *Lies that Bind*, a romance fiction novel, sold on amazon at http://www.amazon.com/Lies-That-Bind-Delinda-McCann/dp/1462898408. And let us not forget our poet in the house, Sharla Shults, author of *Awakenings From Then 'til Now*, newly released in January this year. What better place than Scotland to write about dreams, aye? See all of her works at http://www.sharlashults.com.

Completing our table is Lucretia Ferch, her husband Peter James Taaffe and son Teagan Francis, all from Bremerton, Washington. Lucretia is a fine massage therapist in my home town of Bremerton. Her sister-in-law, Debbie Taaffe Kovach hails from Arizona and is a welcome addition to join our group of authors.

By now you must know that I am in heaven, as we all rejoice in this special celebration of life. As the evening passes into night, we continue our celebration, sharing in good times and sharing our most intimate secrets as only good friends would do.

Yes, I'm riding high, knowing that it wasn't so long ago that such a trip would only have been possible in my dreams. My spirit could never be broken as a child and I did dream of how it would be one day but I had only envisioned it as a fairytale. This is so much better, proving that to never give up is the answer for your dreams to come true.

As if things couldn't get any better, the next morning will see us off to Belfast, Ireland for the second leg of our trip. Now you'd never go to Belfast without touring the great ship Titanic in its rightful home. The sheer size of that majestic beauty is mind boggling but soaking up the history of the tragic loss of so many is a sobering experience not to be forgotten. Before moving on, we still have so many activities on our itinerary...a tour of the Giants Causeway, learning the history of Bushmills Distillery, visiting Castles and spending time just enjoying the company of one another. Aren't we the lucky ones for having a talented massage therapist in our group? After a busy day, our tired muscles need some special attention. Do you think that a glass of Guinness or Bushmills might be a fair exchange to get her to work on her vacation?

After our fabulous visit to Belfast, we're ready to move on to Dublin where there's no end of things to do and places to see. The first stop is Trinity College to see the Book of Kells where we get to view that magnificent library, so steeped in history it'll take your breath away. And what an experience it'll be for the thirteen year old in our group when we visit the Medieval Dublinia to learn the ways of the Vikings. Young Teagen will dazzle us with song as he dons Viking clothes and dances his way to the tower top that overlooks the City of Dublin, where he explains in his own dramatic style, how he would have protected us in those times. Last but not least, we travel an hour north to Carlingford to the Taaffe castle, owned by the Irish relatives of the Taaffes in our group.

Well, I'm not tired yet, are you? Let's take the Hop On Hop Off bus and tour the city of Dublin. We can hop off wherever we wish but our priorities are Dublin Castle, Christ Church and the Temple Bar area to take in the vivid colors. By evening, a Pub Crawl is offered so you can visit the famous traditional establishments which are part of Dublin's history. Getting swept up in the traditional song and dance of long ago will have you falling in love over and over again. I wonder if the pub crawl will include Peter's heritage of the Taaffe Pub but if not, we'll be sure to include it ourselves.

Now isn't this a grand opportunity for the authors in our group who have heritage in this lovely country? Kathleen Boyles, an attorney in Tacoma and Delinda from Gig Harbor, Linda from Ontario, Canada and myself all have Irish roots in our genealogy. What a book we could all write together, but that's another dream. We still have so much to do, including a visit to St. Stephens Green and enjoying a picnic by the ponds as the ducks swim by. I don't believe I've ever used so many modes of transport as I did on the Dublin leg of our trip…bus, rail, horse and trap and of course our good old reliable feet. I think I like my dream far better than any movie could ever tell.

Now for a good night's rest before we pick up the vans that will carry us through the lush countryside on the way to Blarney. Most of the trip will hug the coastline, allowing us to enjoy the sea air and the tranquility that it brings. You already know what that means to me. The view is spectacular with the waves splashing upon the surf and at times, violently against the giant rocks and pounding the shore. Laughter fills our vans as we travel down the ultra-narrow roads with our windows open while trying to avoid the tree branches that seem determined to either gently kiss or slap us on our cheeks.

As we pulled into the parking lot of the Blarney Woollen Mills Hotel, I felt butterflies in my stomach as I anticipated my pre-arranged book signing. We plan on anchoring here for several days, allowing for two days of book signings in the store to promote my book, entitled *Extraordinary Dreams of an Ireland Traveler* and to debut this book. How wonderful it is to be promoting two books in Ireland when only two years ago, they were both still in the planning stages. Then I remind myself that dreams really do come true, even for me.

Now, one does not go to Blarney without shopping for the lovely Irish woollen knits in the largest store in Ireland. The selection is overwhelming and most impressive of all is the Aine Knitwear. Of course, we'll try on Aine's entire line and no doubt, will buy up all available stock to take home and show off. Even more exciting will be getting to meet the designer herself.

There's so much to do in Blarney. When we're not doing the book signing, we'll be off seeing the sights, most notably, the Blarney Castle where we'll get to kiss the Blarney Stone, likely to be the subject of lively chatter for days to come. Other sites include the amazing Cliffs of Moher, Waterford Crystal Factory, Ring of Kerry, City of Cork, the famous English Market and even a visit to the City of Kinsale to savor some of the finest cuisine in the country.

Now here's an interesting tidbit! While traveling through the countryside, we've noticed that many castles are for sale. So aren't we the lucky ones. We have a very learned financial advisor/retirement counselor in our group, Peter James Taaffe, to advise any among us who might decide to dabble in this unique real estate market. Just imagine owning one of these famous castles. Forgive me for a moment while I digress into my planning mode. Let's see now— our castle gift shop absolutely must carry the finest woollens in the land and feature the hand knits of Aine Knitwear front and center! Perhaps we could ask Lucretia's sister-in-law from Arizona to manage it for us. Okay, now the wheels are turning as I see more retirement planning on the horizon.

I'd be remiss if I didn't include a day tour through the Wicklow Mountains where it is said to grow the largest strawberries in all of Ireland. Maybe we'll opt for a rail tour and park the van for a day. Hmmmm – strawberries! What a delightful ending to our extended visit to Blarney.

Next up is a short two day stay in Killarney where we plan to tour the grandest place of all…Muckross House and Gardens in the exquisite Killarney National Park. We may even decide take a boat ride on Lake Killarney but for sure the romantic horse and trap through the park is a must.

Excitement is mounting as we move on to the alluring City of Galway! This leg of our journey is special indeed and where I've made arrangements for all of my author friends to do a major book signing event in the famous Charlie Byrne's Book Store in the heart of the city. I'm told that this is a quaint and very fine place to meet the locals and tourists alike.

I can't begin to count the major tourist attractions in Galway and our cameras must always be close at hand. I do have a confession to

make though. On my first trip, I promised my good friend 'Fungi' the dolphin who lives on the Dingle Peninsula that if ever I returned to Ireland, I would make a special effort to revisit him. Others can join me if they wish but this is a 'must do' item on my agenda.

Traveling along Galway Bay is an unforgettable treat. We must stop at Salt Hill to drink in its many charms, not the least of which is its memorable seashore which is so reminiscent of home. As we did on our first trip to Ireland, Doug and I will walk the beach barefoot, hand-in-hand while we appreciate the gentle breezes brushing against our face and feel the sea at our heels. I can't help but wonder though, how anyone could dive into those cold waters with any degree of comfort. I think we'll just stick with the sand between our toes!

Now that we're relaxed from the balmy sea air, we're heading for the Promenade to sit and chat with people on the many benches that line the walkway. We might even stop to make some new canine friends in memory of our precious Sandy, who passed away while I was writing this very chapter. Our sweet chocolate Lab would have loved it here as beach walking was her favorite thing to do. Oh, did I mention that as we walk along the Promenade, it is customary to kick the wall and make a wish just as all the locals do?

"Ok, are you ready for the next part? You should be because I saved the best for last." Here's where we plan to stay.

Atlantic Heights Bed and Breakfast

Soon we arrive at our won-
derful B & B, where we'll
spend our entire stay and
only minutes from Galway.
Oh my, that photograph
from Madeline sure is
wonderful but this is one
instance where a photo
does not speak louder than

Our Host: Madeline and Robbie Mitchell

words. This charming home has all the appeal of a southern mansion with its tall, sleek lines and dormers painted in a pristine cream
to capture the sunlight. Especially memorable is the softly colored
trim and the marine blue sun porch to blend with the color of the
sea. Just a moment while I get my camera! Okay, I'm back and busy

snapping pictures of brightly colored flower pots in the windows next to the outdoor seating on the verandah. You can bet that I'll while away some hours in those inviting chairs while I admire two of God's greatest gifts…the sea and my wonderful partner in life.

Still caught up in our dream world, we finally get to meet our wonderful hosts, Madeline and Robbie. After a friendly welcome, Madeline takes us to our rooms to freshen up and unwind for a bit. Oh my goodness, were we in for a treat. The ocean side view combined with the scent of freshly cut flowers on the dressers was enough to lull me into fantasy land. To complete the picture, add crisply ironed linens, a fruit basket and to top it all off, a staff member drops in with two glasses and a bottle of champagne, and on ice yet which is a rare treat in Ireland. When we emerge from our quarters, she politely ushers us into another charming room where we are served hot tea and freshly baked scones with a special strawberry jam Robbie had prepared especially for us.

Feeling refreshed and rejuvenated, we are now ready for our evening activities. We'll definitely venture out later for dinner at a restaurant we were referred to and take a leisurely stroll along the beach. After that, Doug and I hope to spend some quality time with Madeline to get to know her better and to share the highlights of our trip. Yes, we will become fast friends on this, our very first day.

After enjoying the evening sunset, we set off for O'Grady's Restaurant at the harbor in Barna where Madeline so kindly made our dinner reservations, only a couple of miles down the road. She must have let them know about my relationship with the sea because they seated us by the window with the best view in the house. We are joined by all ten of our friends, in front of whom Doug and I will share our vows of recommitment to one another over a sparkling glass of wine. Don't tell anyone but we saved our champagne for a private celebration on our balcony before we retire for the night. How could love possibly get better than this?

Our next day begins with an award winning breakfast prepared by Madeline and staff and served inside the conservatory where the lovely flowers are the crowning touch to the atmosphere. The option is to enjoy room service but who'd ever want to miss out on this wonderful experience.

Our next day is all set and again thanks to Madeline's energy and thoughtfulness, a book signing has been arranged for us at Charlie Byrne's Book Shop in Galway (http://www.charliebyrne.com/index. php?PHPSESSID=9e5d321b66632f5b9b9260f7c0dc3626). Now I ask you, does life get any better than this? I'm married to the man of my dreams, have a daughter that any mother would be proud of and a magnificent home away from home in romantic Ireland. All of my life, I longed to be a writer but was discouraged by my mother as being a 'no talent wannabe' yet here I am, at a book signing in a world class bookstore an ocean away from home. I hate to say I told you so mother, but I'm living my dream and I did it all without you. At long last, I'm free.

Oh how I hate to leave Galway-Salt Hill and the new friends we've made here. Madeline and Robbie from Atlantic Heights B & B and Charley, Vinny and Carmel of Charlie Byrne's Book Shop. Thanks to each of you for making our stay here a total delight and a major success story for our books.

Now we're off to Limerick for two days, our last stop before heading home. Being the year of the Gathering, everything here has been booked well in advance so we were fortunate to have our reservations confirmed before we left home. We didn't get to spend enough time here when we visited in 2011 and we hope to make up for it this time by spending an entire day at the Bunratty Castle and Folk Park and top the day off with the castle banquet celebration, complete with traditional Irish dancing with lively entertaining music. We enjoyed the Medieval Banquet on our first trip but this night promises to be a cultural event not soon to be forgotten.

We end our night in our rooms at the romantic Bunratty Castle Hotel where we pack our belongings for our long trip home.

I invite you to enjoy a few photos from our last trip to Bunratty. You'll see for yourself why this is the perfect ending for a dream come true.

Now how would you like to be greeted in this manner for dinner?

And entertained by the friendly Bunratty performers.

Or simply stroll through the Folk Park town center. It's all there waiting for you to enjoy with so much to see. Why not turn your dreams into reality?

As you know, I've been a dreamer my entire life, forever contemplating the 'what ifs' and wondering where my life's journey will lead me and now those dreams have all come true. Ireland, you'll forever be in my heart alongside my darling husband, who is my soul mate for life.

"Now, didn't I tell you that
I was a dreamer?"

About the Author

Rosemary "Mamie" Adkins Is An Author, Speaker, Survivor And Master Of Her Own Destiny.

I was born Rosemary Jeannette Hazen Adkins and spent most of my childhood in Houston, Texas. When I left Texas with my family, we moved to Las Vegas where I graduated from Bishop Gorman High School in 1965. After graduation, my family moved to Redding,

California where we resided for about six months before I fled the state and family home, just weeks prior to becoming the legal age of eighteen. From there on, I seemed to be restless and moved around until I found a happy place to be in Eugene, Oregon.

My childhood was not the happiest as I dealt with the challenges of abuse that would impact my life for decades to come. I found great peace walking the ocean's beaches or swimming in the Gulf. In fact, the beach is where I worked through my devastating issues of self-doubt, fear and loneliness and where I often returned to help me through the process of resurrecting my most painful memories to share with you in this book. It was where I drew the strength to defeat the monsters that haunted my soul…a special place where I would always find peace.

Although I had gained my independence, abuse continued to follow me wherever I went, only now it was because of my own bad choices. Ever in search of the love and security that I had never known, it took many failed relationships and two bad marriages before I learned the lessons that life was trying to teach me.

My blessing finally arrived when I met and married my wonderful husband, Douglas Earl Adkins. Kecia, who I had adopted earlier, became the light of his life and we are still enjoying peace and happiness today, after twenty-five years of wedded bliss.

Now I had the picture perfect life that I had always hoped for but serious health issues would intervene to disrupt my serenity. I have faced the raging challenges of Diabetes for the past twenty-seven years and have survived at least two life and death experiences. At its worst, Diabetes can be a form of abuse in its own right and one that is not always easy to control. I have been fortunate to have the devoted help of my husband and daughter who keep me on the straight and narrow when it comes to taking good care of my health.

For many years, I had dreamt of writing this book so that I might help others to learn from my experience, but is was far easier said than done. Many of my memories were too painful to relive and others were buried so deep that my memory was fraught with vast voids that I was unable to fill. It didn't help that my Mother's abuse continued to the end of her life, leaving my self-confidence in tatters. As I write this, her words still echo in my ears, "Mamie, you're too stupid to get anywhere with your writing." Now that Mother has passed on to wherever she ended up, I chose to write my story anyway.

What a wonderful surprise it was to discover that music could free my soul to get my words onto paper. I had met *Charles Suniga*, the pianist and composer of some of the world's most enchanting music. His album 'Moments of Peace' played softly in the background, while allowing me to reach deep inside to reveal the true *'Reflections of Mamie'*. "Thank you Charles."

Now that I've finally emptied my soul of a lifetime of pain, I've been able to put those tragic memories back in my past where they belong. That dark hole that was my past has given up the last of its secrets and I am no longer held prisoner by it. I am free at last to live my life fully, unencumbered by sad memories. Now, if I can help at least one person with my story, it will all have been worth it.

I am a mother, wife, sister and a friend to many people. In addition, I have, with the help of my husband and daughter, organized and established an American Diabetes Association Chapter in our state and advocated for Diabetics worldwide. A story I wrote about how my family and friends had impacted my life led to winning a trip to Washington DC for myself and my husband. There, in the presence of several leaders in the US government, I was presented with an award at the Kennedy Center during a special concert by Gladys Knight. I was also presented with the 'Unsung Hero' award by our local newspaper, the Kitsap Sun, for my volunteer work in the area we live in. That celebration was held in The Admiral Theater before family and an audience of well-wishers.

Now in my senior years, my dream of writing my first book became a reality in 2011. *Extraordinary Dreams of An Ireland Traveler'* is an invaluable account of our personal travels throughout Ireland, complete with a wealth of historic detail and an in-depth guide to savings for the tourist. The rest is history. I gained tremendous insight into the world of publishing and the courage to complete *'Reflections of Mamie'* which had been sixteen years in the making. This, my second book, will be distributed by summer 2013.

My dear friends, I cannot thank you enough for taking the time to read my memoirs, and share an inside account of the abuse I suffered behind closed doors. My fondest wish is that other abuse victims will prevail over their own tragic pasts by learning to make life choices that will stop the pattern of abuse in its tracks. It can be done. My story reveals how I made it happen for me. You will find your true destiny if you never give up.

CPSIA information can be obtained at www.ICGtesting.com
Printed in the USA
LVOW02s1650081013

356004LV00020B/44/P

9 781938 686467